NEW OXFORD ENGLISH SERIES
General Editor: A. NORMAN JEFFARES

WORDSWORTH

SELECTED POETRY
AND PROSE

Chosen and edited by

JOHN BUTT

REGIUS PROFESSOR OF
RHETORIC AND ENGLISH LITERATURE
UNIVERSITY OF EDINBURGH

OXFORD UNIVERSITY PRESS

Oxford University Press, Ely House, London W. 1

GLASGOW NEW YORK TORONTO MELBOURNE WELLINGTON
CAPE TOWN IBADAN NAIROBI DAR ES SALAAM LUSAKA ADDIS ABABA
DELHI BOMBAY CALCUTTA MADRAS KARACHI LAHORE DACCA
KUALA LUMPUR SINGAPORE HONG KONG TOKYO

© *Oxford University Press 1964*

First published 1964
Reprinted 1965, 1969, 1971, 1973

Printed in Great Britain
at the University Press, Oxford
by Vivian Ridler
Printer to the University

CONTENTS

CONTENTS

INTRODUCTION

WHEN Wordsworth began in 1798 to write the great philosophical poem that he was never to complete, he thought it
was a reasonable thing to take review of his own mind and
'examine how far Nature and Education had qualified him
for such an employment'. Accordingly he decided 'to record,
in verse, the origin and progress of his powers'. That poem is
The Prelude, and extracts from it stand first in this selection
because it is autobiographical. But since it was intended as a
review of his mind, Wordsworth does not tell us all that it
concerns us to know. Though he records that he was born in
the north of England, he does not think fit to mention that
he came of professional stock, who owned some little
landed property. He does not tell us that he lost both mother
and father at an early age, that he was entrusted to the care of
unsympathetic relatives with a load of debts owed to him by
his father's employer, the Earl of Lonsdale, and that so powerful a nobleman could not be forced by law to recognize the
elementary rights of man. Perhaps he did not recognize how
much these early experiences affected him; and perhaps he
underestimated what he derived from his formal education at
school and university, of which he offers no detailed account,
though we shall see that his reading in the classics and the
modern literatures of Europe was wide. We may also rest
assured that he was affected by the Newtonian philosophy that
he encountered at Cambridge. He writes at length about his
momentous visit to France, and we may see from his account
by what means his sentimental interest in the Revolution was
converted into one that was practical, reasoned, and even doctrinaire; but he does not allude to the love affair with Annette

Vallon that seems to have made no important contribution to his mental development. He has much to say about the mental and spiritual perplexities of the years immediately following his return to England; but he says nothing about his resistance to his relatives' expectations that he should pursue a career in the church or in the law courts. He himself seems to have vaguely contemplated a living from journalism until a legacy gave him the means of making a modest home for himself and his devoted sister Dorothy, first at Racedown in Dorset, then at Alfoxden in Somerset (to which he moved so as to be nearer his new-found friend Coleridge), and finally at Grasmere in Westmorland.

His verse narrative does not take us much beyond his return to England, and of the fifty years of life that were to be his after his settlement in Grasmere there is little that needs saying. They were years of hard work in his chosen vocation, with public recognition growing as the sources of his inspiration began to fail: the signal honour of the poet-laureateship awarded to him in 1843 has a peculiar appropriateness to the man who had written the sonnets dedicated to National Independence and Liberty (pp. 157–62) forty years before. They were years of domestic happiness and of distressing bereavements. They brought him little bodily enfeeblement—he could still walk from morning to night at the age of 76—and if they brought some traces of mental ossification, they left him the moments of insight to which the last poems in this volume bear witness.

II

One of the earliest passages written for the great philosophical poem was a draft of the 'Prospectus' printed at the beginning of this selection. In those lines he declares his theme—Man, Nature, and Human Life—the theme of all his poetry. The order is important. Man comes first, and the young poet promises that he will speak of 'moral strength, and intellectual Power', and of 'joy in widest commonalty spread'. He will also show how Man and Nature are related, 'how exquisitely the individual Mind . . . to the external World is fitted', and conversely how the external world is fitted to the comprehension of the mind. But it is 'the Mind of Man' that is to be his 'haunt' and the main region of his song, and more particularly it is the exploration of his own mind that is promised. The *Poems* of 1807 received for a sub-title, 'Moods of my own Mind'; and when Mrs. Wordsworth came to choose a title for the long poem her husband had left unpublished at his death, she added to her chosen title *The Prelude* the admirably descriptive sub-title, 'The Growth of a Poet's Mind'.

But Wordsworth would have been the first to protest that the mind is not the whole of Man. The affections have their great place, too; and looking back upon what he had written at the age of 65, he told a friend that if his writings were to last, it would be mainly owing to this characteristic: 'they will please for the single cause, "that we have all of us one human heart"'.

His own mind, the mind he knew best, is the subject of his longest poem; but ranged around that great edifice, like 'little cells, oratories, and sepulchral recesses', as he described them, are those shorter poems, in many of which he explores the minds and affections of other people. Together they give him a claim to be considered not so much as a philosophical but as a psychological poet.

From the time of *Lyrical Ballads* onwards he liked to choose for presentation episodes which characterize some state of being. When Lewis Carroll perpetrated a happy parody of Wordsworth in the sequel to *Alice in Wonderland*, he picked unerringly upon certain prominent characteristics of these

shorter poems, the record of a brief encounter, and the in-
quiring—not to say inquisitive, or even inquisitorial—habit of
the poet:

> I'll tell thee everything I can:
>   There's little to relate.
> I saw an aged aged man,
>   A-sitting on a gate.
> 'Who are you, aged man?' I said.
>   'And how is it you live?'
> And his answer trickled through my head
>   Like water through a sieve.

Lewis Carroll's aim was directed at 'Resolution and Independence' (p. 145); but just so, the poet had recorded in *Lyrical
Ballads* his encounters with Simon Lee the old huntsman
(p. 88), with Little Edward in 'Anecdote for Fathers' (p. 91),
with the Little Cottage Girl in 'We are Seven' (p. 94), and
with a farmer bearing a lamb in his arms in 'The Last of the
Flock' (p. 102). In subsequent volumes there were to be similar encounters, notably in 'The Sailor's Mother' (p. 141)
and 'Beggars' (p. 143). In a few of these poems there are passages of narrative; thus the farmer in 'The Last of the Flock'
relates the story of the misfortunes which have brought him
to his present pass; and in others it is necessary for us to know
what the man used to be so that we may appreciate what he
has now become: thus we are told of Simon Lee that there
was a time when

> He all the country could outrun,
> Could leave both man and horse behind,

though now he is 'the weakest in the village'. But what
Wordsworth is at pains to stress in all these poems is the
existing state of each of the men, women, and children he
meets in these encounters. Speculation about their future is

never entertained, for they are to be preserved as they are as representations of moral principles, frequently of moral principles which had been overlooked. Thus Godwin and other doctrinaire philosophers of the time come in for some hard knocks, even though they may not be mentioned by name. Thus 'The Last of the Flock' declares that the ownership of property is not soul-destroying, not a cause of vice, as Godwin had said, but rather a buttress of self-respect; and in 'Anecdote for Fathers' he shows that lying is not always unnatural and vicious, as Godwin had said, but rather the natural resort of children who are pressed too far; while 'Simon Lee' helps us to recognize that gratitude is not simply a cringing to wealth and power, as Godwin had said, but a spontaneous and pathetic effusion of the heart.

The underlying moral principle is even more clearly presented in 'The Old Cumberland Beggar' (p. 76), a poem written as a rebuke to those political economists who wished to sweep away both begging and almsgiving. A more feeble, helpless, and seemingly purposeless life it would be difficult to imagine than that which Wordsworth describes in the first sixty-five lines of his poem; yet the old man is not to be deemed useless:

> 'Tis Nature's law
> That none, the meanest of created things,
> Of forms created the most vile and brute,
> The dullest or most noxious, should exist
> Divorced from good.

The beggar subsists only upon what the villagers give him. That they are ready to give to him at all shows that their hearts are kept open to acts of love, which otherwise would 'by sure steps resign / To selfishness and cold oblivious cares'. Without him there would be no means of keeping alive 'the kindly mood in hearts' made slow to feel by the lapse of

years. That we should do good to others is part of the moral
law; and without the beggar no opportunities would exist
for the abject poor. Thus Wordsworth sees the beggar as one
of the binding forces in rural society; this is one of the views
of Man and Society that he had promised us. And if it seems
hard upon the beggar that he should exist simply in order to
keep other men's hearts warm, it would be harder still to
send him to the Workhouse, and make him economically
useful to society. No, let him rather have his freedom in that
state which he shares with the aged leech-gatherer, a settled
state of quietness, beyond any sharp sense of want, beyond
even resignation. So too, in 'Animal Tranquillity and Decay'
(p. 83), the beggar

> is insensibly subdued
> To settled quiet: he is one by whom
> All effort seems forgotten; one to whom
> Long patience hath such mild composure given,
> That patience now doth seem a thing of which
> He hath no need. He is by nature led
> To peace so perfect that the young behold
> With envy, what the Old Man hardly feels.

That is Wordsworth's retort to the imagined objection that
it is hard upon the beggar; and the same retort may be read into
the episode at the end of *The Prelude*, Book IV (p. 59),
where the young poet meets one summer night a gaunt old
soldier propped against a milestone, and finds him calm and
steady in demeanour. These old men have something from
which the young may learn, and even something which the
young may envy. Different names are found for it: resolution,
independence, patience, endurance, composure, and that
settled quietness which the young Wordsworth seems to have
been abnormally conscious of lacking (p. 44). It is found
once again in 'Michael' (p. 119), after the old man has learned

the news of his son's disgrace. He too quietly endures, performing his customary tasks, and showing in only one detail of behaviour (p. 133) the desolation that had come upon him.

These are case-histories that Wordsworth has set before us for our edification, of which one merit they have in common is their changelessness. The attitude of the poet is deeply sympathetic, but it is that of spectator. He has a clinical interest in these cases, as he gathers us his students around him to anatomize parental love in 'Michael' and 'The Idiot Boy', to display the workings of the superstitious mind in 'Goody Blake and Harry Gill' (p. 84) and 'The Thorn', to show in 'We are Seven' (p. 94) how intuitively may be grasped the fact of the indestructibility at death of essential being. These are all objective studies from the case book of a psychological poet, and they are essentially static, comfortingly static, for the Solitary Reaper (p. 167) sings as though her song 'could have no ending'. She is equated with other singing creatures, the nightingale and the cuckoo, and is thus a part almost of the indestructible world of nature, just as the leech-gatherer, equated with huge stone, sea-beast, and cloud, seems in the poet's eye to 'pace / About the weary moors continually'. They are static in the same sense as Keats's nightingale is static, an immortal bird 'not born for death'. Neither poet is so foolish as to imagine that the individual nightingale, the individual leech-gatherer, and the individual reaper will not die. Each poet is declaring that he has for one important moment recognized them as belonging in type to the imperishable world of nature.

III

These poems are essentially, comfortingly, and edifyingly static; but there is another group of poems, essentially dynamic, that may be called poems of becoming. The first in time is the

'Lines Written a Few Miles above Tintern Abbey'. Whereas the importance of such poems as 'The Solitary Reaper' and 'The Old Cumberland Beggar' is that the central figure exists outside and beyond considerations of time, the Tintern Abbey 'Lines' (see p. 110) are placed firmly and emphatically in time:

> Five years have passed; five summers, with the length
> Of five long winters! and again I hear
> These waters ...

The framework of the argument depends upon a comparison of what the poet was five years ago (at the age of twenty-three, incidentally) with what he is now; and still further measures of time are indicated by reaching back to recall 'the coarser pleasures of my boyish days, / And their glad animal movements', and by looking forward, not indeed to a radically altered state, but to one where joy will have been added to joy. The principal contrast lies between twenty-three and twenty-eight; the intervening years have been years of development, and the poet is drawing up an interim balance sheet of profit and loss. Twenty-three was an age of still largely animal delights, or at any rate of purely physical responses: when 'like a roe' he 'bounded o'er the mountains', when 'the mountain, and the deep and gloomy wood' were to him 'an appetite'. This was a time of 'aching joys' and 'dizzy raptures', when the eye (of all the senses) was predominant. And now that time has been succeeded by another time characterized by more sober responses, where the power of reflection supervenes. So far as the balance sheet is concerned there is felt to be abundant recompense for the loss of purely physical response. Precisely what has been gained is difficult to define, but perhaps these things. First, the power of recollection, such as Wordsworth also mentions in 'I wandered lonely as a cloud' (p. 153), the ability of returning to these

sources of his power in moods of dejection, and so of trans-
forming those moods. He paid tribute to this power in his
theory of the origin of poetry expounded in the preface to
Lyrical Ballads (p. 213), where he explains how it arises from
emotion recollected in tranquillity. Not all his poetry was
composed in this way; the opening lines of *The Prelude*, the
Tintern Abbey 'Lines', and 'Written in March' were all composed immediately after the events they celebrate without
any intervening periods of digestion. On the other hand we
know how long the intervals were between the experiences
which prompted 'I wandered lonely as a cloud' and
'Resolution and Independence' and the composition of those
poems; and it is part of the interest of Dorothy Wordsworth's
journal that she records not merely the intervals of time
but the original experiences, or something very like them (see
p. 214). Her records give us some notion of how the experiences matured in the poet's mind, and of what the process
of composition involved.

Secondly, he had gained an important new mystical experience, the stages of which follow—doubtless without any
awareness on Wordsworth's part—the classical stages recognized by Plotinus: first, the physical quiet:

> the motion of our human blood
> Almost suspended, we are laid asleep in body;

then the new spiritual awareness: we

> become a living soul;
> While with an eye made quiet by the power
> Of harmony, and the deep power of joy,
> We see into the life of things;

and finally the mystic's attainment of a vision of the absolute,
the principal characteristic of this vision being a recognition
of a new relationship between all created things. The spirit

> Whose dwelling is the light of setting suns,
> And the round ocean and the living air,

dwells also 'in the mind of man', and impels

> All thinking things, all objects of all thought,
> And rolls through all things.

Wordsworth seems to imply that this mystical experience had not been his when he was last at Tintern in 1793. Something very like it, however, is described in the additions made to *An Evening Walk* at Keswick in 1794, where he speaks of the mind being 'Rapt into worlds beyond the reign of sense'; and the pre-eminent example of this experience had come to him when crossing the Alps in the summer of 1790. The experience is not discussed in *Descriptive Sketches* of 1793, which deals with this tour. Indeed it was not until another eleven years had passed, fourteen years after the experience itself, that he was able to find adequate words for the experience in *The Prelude*, Book VI (p. 64). He there recalls the physical slackening which ensued when the peasant told him he had crossed the Alps. This was followed, as in the Tintern Abbey 'Lines', by the increased spiritual awareness, which brought a new vision of the organization of Nature:

> when the light of sense
> Goes out, but with a flash that has revealed
> The invisible world.

The vision, vouchsafed as he walked down the Pass, is of close relationship once more, even of unity; and the passage in which he conveys it (p. 64, ll. 624–40) is one of Wordsworth's grandest affirmations. Such vision was abundant recompense for the loss of aching joys and dizzy raptures; but the experience of the mystics is that these visitations are exhausting. So Wordsworth seems to have thought, and in the 'Ode to

Duty' (p. 186) we see him bearing witness to this. He had been one who relied upon 'the genial sense of youth', for whom love had been 'an unerring light' and joy 'its own security': he had been content to rely solely upon the immediacy and the freshness of his response to experience. But there comes the moment of recognition that this is not enough (ll. 37–40):

> Me this unchartered freedom tires;
> I feel the weight of chance-desires:
> My hopes no more must change their name,
> I long for a repose that ever is the same.

It is a sad confession. But as in the Tintern Abbey 'Lines' there is a balance to be struck. Against the loss there is to be reckoned some recompense. In the service of duty there is gladness. Required tasks are not all performed listlessly. Do not the angels of God rejoice to perform his bidding? And is not that patently true of his other creatures?

> Flowers laugh before thee on their beds
> And fragrance in thy footing treads;
> Thou dost preserve the stars from wrong;
> And the most ancient heavens, through Thee, are fresh and
>   strong.

Defeat has been almost miraculously averted, and profit snatched out of the very jaws of loss.

That also is the impression gained from another of these poems of becoming, the 'Ode: Intimations of Immortality'. In this poem the scales are weighted still further. The first four stanzas, written two years before the remainder of the ode, emphasize the sense of loss, and the hypothesis of pre-existence which follows only serves to intensify it. The child is no longer dismissed with a phrase about his 'coarser pleasures', as he was treated in the Tintern Abbey 'Lines': now he is addressed—much to Coleridge's impatience—as 'Mighty

prophet... glorious in the might / Of heaven-born freedom.'
Far from finding abundant recompense for what is lost, what
now we find is 'joy that in our embers / Is something that doth
live'. The scales are weighted; yet Wordsworth contrives a
rescue even from this desperate situation:

> We will grieve not, rather find
> Strength in what remains behind;

that is to say, strength both in what survives from childhood,
and in what is found to compensate; in the primal sympathy
between the child and nature that still survives, in 'the soothing thoughts that spring / Out of human suffering'.

It is presumably those soothing thoughts about human
suffering that are provoked at the end of the poem by 'the
meanest flower that blows'. A similar association of human
suffering and the natural creation is found in the Tintern
Abbey 'Lines', when Wordsworth writes of hearing in
nature oftentimes 'the still, sad music of humanity'; and again
we find it in 'Lines Written in Early Spring' (p. 99):

> To her fair works did Nature link
> The human soul that through me ran;
> And much it grieved my heart to think
> What man has made of man.

This may perhaps be linked with those associations of the
shepherd and the mountains described at length in *The
Prelude*, Book VIII (p. 65), and with what was said earlier
about the leech-gatherer and the old beggar. It is precisely here
that we may detect some change in attitude in the next of
these poems of becoming, the 'Elegiac Stanzas suggested by
a Picture of Peele Castle, in a Storm' (p. 189), written a year
later than the two Odes. In this poem, as in the others examined, two states are presented for contrast, the young poet
and the poet who has been through the experience of suffering.

There is a touch of compassion expressed for the youth who in 'the fond illusion' of his heart could have painted a picture of Elysian quiet. But there has been a change, involving losses and gains:

> I have submitted to a new control:
> A power is gone, which nothing can restore;
> A deep distress hath humanised my Soul.

Recognizing the importance Wordsworth always attaches to the word 'power', we can gauge the severity of the loss; but once more there is compensation, in that he finds his soul has been 'humanised' by a deep distress, the death at sea of his dearly loved brother, John.

He had already spoken of hearing 'the still, sad music of humanity'; but now this 'deep distress' has made him recognize that all his previous explorations of the human mind and heart were a little too clinical, were made by a spectator who, however sympathetic, was a trifle detached in his point of view. And so he bids farewell to

> the heart that lives alone,
> Housed in a dream, at distance from the Kind!

A closer involvement in the human predicament is what he now promises himself, and the poem ends in much the same chastened and restrained mood as the 'Ode to Duty', with a welcome to 'fortitude, and patient cheer'.

There is at least one more poem which belongs to this group, the Ode 'Composed upon an Evening of Extraordinary Splendour and Beauty' (p. 202). It is an epilogue to the others. Nearly twenty years after the Tintern Abbey 'Lines', his mystical experience was momentarily and miraculously renewed. For three stanzas he glories in the visitation; and then, in what we have come to recognize as his custom, he compares an earlier state when these visitations were more frequent with his later state. The sense of loss is strongly felt: he recalls a light that was 'full early lost, and fruitlessly deplored'. What has taken its place is peace and calmness, a contentedness (apparently) to keep to the paths of Duty.

> 'Tis past, the visionary splendour fades;
> And night approaches with her shades.

These poems of becoming present a subjective impression of the poet's most individual and precious experience. They take their place as cells and oratories off the great central edifice, the longest and most important of the poems of becoming, *The Prelude*. But they also offer an assessment of the experience, with a different estimate at different periods. In 1798, when he could not know that the experience would be impermanent, it was supremely valuable, and its value was wistfully recalled in 1817 after years of living without it. In the spring of 1804, when the 'Ode to Duty' was written and the 'Intimations' Ode completed, he was still living in the bright memory of the experience and finding compensations for its loss, compensations in the value of which he felt assured when he came the following year to write the 'Elegiac Stanzas'.

We are tempted to dismiss the compensations, because the waning of the experience seems to have brought about the death of the poet's imagination, and that is what principally concerns us. But the compensations do at least suggest that Wordsworth attained in himself the patience and settled quiet whose virtues he had so often sung in his great poetic years, and which he acclaimed with stoical satisfaction in *The Excursion* (p. 197). A lesson in morals has been purchased, but at a heavy price. An unsympathetic reader might call it the price of growing up.

IV

For most critics of Wordsworth there is a strong temptation to linger over the fascinations of what he has to say, and
to neglect his poetic craftsmanship. He himself has directed
attention to one aspect of his craftsmanship, his poetic diction,
by what he said about it in the Preface to *Lyrical Ballads* (see
p. 210); but except to critics looking for a convenient club to
smite eighteenth-century poets with, it has not proved a
satisfying topic of discussion, chiefly because it is so patently
at odds with much of the best of his poetry. Furthermore, by
laying claim to novelty, or at any rate to reform, in this aspect
of his work, Wordsworth has had the effect of withdrawing
attention from the strong measure of traditionalism in his
verse. So far as verse forms were concerned it was never
Wordsworth's habit to invent. The popular ballad of humble
life was in use throughout the eighteenth century. The
Miltonic sonnet, though rare before 1770, had enjoyed a
great vogue in the eighties and nineties. Thomson in the
seventeen-twenties and Akenside in the seventeen-forties had
accustomed readers to the use of blank verse for meditative
poetry. In his use of the ode, too, Wordsworth was a tradi-
tionalist: though he wrote elsewhere with disrespect of Gray's
poetry, he dictated a note to say that the 'Ode to Duty' was
modelled on Gray's 'Ode to Adversity', and the model for
the 'Intimations' Ode was the loose form of Pindaric devised
by Cowley, and used with great success by Dryden in the
'Ode for St. Cecilia's Day' and 'Alexander's Feast'.

Wordsworth in fact was a rather bookish poet. He can
often be watched turning to earlier masters to solve some of
his literary problems. Thus the choice of Dryden's Pindaric
for the 'Intimations' Ode was dictated by his need for a form
which would permit the abrupt transition ('Our birth is but

a sleep and a forgetting'), and would naturalize the exclamatory address ('Mighty Prophet! Seer blest!' 'Then sing, ye Birds, sing, sing a joyous song!'), and, more important still, a form in which it was customary for the verse to respond with different measures to the flickering of the poet's mood. The Pindaric Ode had been used to produce effects like these for over a century, though rarely if ever for a poem at once meditative as well as lyrical. In this respect for the old poetic kinds, Wordsworth shows himself content to continue in eighteenth-century traditions.

He is bookish not only in his approach to a literary problem, but often in what he expects of his reader. Readers of Milton, Pope, and Gray, like readers of T. S. Eliot in this century, were accustomed to a certain allusiveness in their authors. They were encouraged to listen for echoes of previous poets, for the echo of a word or phrase, perhaps even for a parody of a famous passage, or for a parody of a recognized manner of writing. The reader of Wordsworth must be almost equally alert. He will often make an allusion which he must have expected his readers to pick up; there is an instance in the first extract (p. 39, l. 23). One of many other instances occurs in *The Prelude*, Book I, l. 246, where he describes himself wrestling with the difficulties of poetical composition, and complaining that humility or modesty 'Locks every function up in blank reserve'. Whether wittingly or unwittingly, he must have had in mind a passage from one of Pope's *Imitations of Horace* (Ep. I. i, ll. 39, 40), where Pope complains in identical terms of time that has been wasted:

> So slow th' unprofitable Moments roll,
> That lock up all the Functions of my soul.

These echoes give such poetry as this a bookish flavour, and their recognition offers the reader a sophisticated pleasure.

There is also parody, the mockery of the grand style brought about by using it in inappropriate contexts. This had been a favourite eighteenth-century pastime played at the expense of the epic or of Milton's blank verse; and Wordsworth plays it too on suitable occasions. Thus he seems to have recognized, justly, that it was undesirable to maintain his theme and his verse in *The Prelude* at their sublimest level throughout; and accordingly he devised several episodes at a deliberately lower pitch. A notable instance of this is the third book, in which he speaks of his undergraduate days at Cambridge and treats them as Cowper might have done in a deliberately mock-heroic tone—a tone entirely suitable for the transformation of this northern rustic into the almost cosmopolitan society of a university in the south (p. 56). But out of this Cowper-like mockery he can soar to the true sublime when his subject requires, as for example when he looks out of his bedroom window in St. John's towards Trinity, and recalls the noble statue of Sir Isaac Newton in the ante-chapel. A similar instance occurs in the first book (p. 49), where the poet recalls the indoor games played as a child on winter evenings; and with Pope's game of ombre in *The Rape of the Lock* not far from the front of his mind he treats us to a mock-heroic description of the well-worn, grubby, greasy, and now incomplete pack of cards he used. The mockery is then abruptly dismissed as he turns in the last lines of the verse paragraph to describe in soaring verse the winter scene outside the cottage, which contrasts with the cosy interior. The most effective example of this deliberately contrived contrast in verse styles is the 'Song at the Feast of Brougham Castle', written in 1807. Two years previously, in 1805, Walter Scott had published with immense success *The Lay of the Last Minstrel*, in which he imagines a border minstrel brought to the Duchess of Buccleuch at the end of the seventeenth century to recite to her the noble deeds of her ancestors. The greater part of Scott's poem consists of the lay recited by the minstrel in the Duchess's state apartment, of which the predominating measure is a rapid octosyllabic in rhyming couplets. Wordsworth adapts these octosyllabics to tell what *his* minstrel sang when the banished Lord Clifford was restored in 1485 to the estates of his ancestors, after spending twenty-four years in hiding as a shepherd. The minstrel sings an impassioned song of greeting to the shepherd lord, and prophesies the great martial deeds he will surely perform; and his manner, if not precisely Scott's, is close enough to remind us of the *Lay*. Then what happens? Is the minstrel's prophecy fulfilled? It is surely one of the most electrifying moments in Wordsworth's poetry when he brushes aside Walter Scott and his octosyllabics to speak, in his own gravely measured tread, the doctrine one never seems to tire in hearing from him (p. 177).

'A selection of the real language of men in a state of vivid sensation' was the phrase substituted in the Preface of 1800 (see p. 210) for what had appeared in the Advertisement of 1798 for the language Wordsworth said he intended to present. In 1798 he had declared that *Lyrical Ballads* 'were written chiefly with a view to ascertain how far the language of conversation in the middle and lower classes of society is adapted to the purposes of poetical pleasure'. By that sentence he did not wish to convey that he was to experiment with what distinguishes rustic speech from other speech: that he never attempts. But there are many passages in *Lyrical Ballads* where his aim seems to be to recover not the grossness of rustic speech, but the baldness of everyday speech. This is apparent in 'Anecdote for Fathers', 'We are Seven', and 'Goody Blake and Harry Gill'. Perhaps he hoped to startle his readers with the language of the broadside ballads; perhaps he meant to tease them. But the presence of the Tintern Abbey

'Lines' in the same volume shows that his statements on poetic diction are insufficient to describe his practice, whether we attend to the earlier statement about 'the language of conversation in the middle and lower classes of society' or the later revised statement about the 'selection of the real language of men in a state of vivid sensation'. Neither statement accounts satisfactorily for the exalted language of the Tintern Abbey 'Lines' and the 'Intimations' Ode. What was needed was a statement which recognized two kinds of poetic language used often, though not invariably, in close association with each other. The baldness of the language of conversation is unmitigated in such a poem as 'Goody Blake and Harry Gill'. It is not always unmitigated. The appeal of such a poem as 'The Sailor's Mother' (p. 141) lies partly in the contrast implied between the majestic dignity of her appearance and the simple language in which she expresses her pathetic situation. In a note dictated many years later Wordsworth recorded the spot where he had met the woman, and added: 'Her appearance was exactly as here described, and such was her account nearly to the letter.' Of many other poems, such as 'Simon Lee', 'The Idiot Boy', and 'Stepping Westward' (p. 166), he has recorded that words attributed to speakers in the poem were the words actually used in real life, as though in justification of his theory. But perhaps the true justification is of a different kind, made critically long before his time.

In the preface to his translation of Longinus *On the Sublime* (1674) Boileau distinguishes between the true sublime and the sublime style. The sublime style affects many words, he says, but the true sublime consists in the shortest and simplest expression: thus 'The sovereign arbiter of Nature with one word created Light' may be sublime in style; but 'God said, "Let there be light, and there was light" ' is the true sublime. He also recalls a passage in the *Horace* of Corneille, where Old

Horace expresses his sense of shame at the news of the battle in which two of his sons had died and the third had fled. When asked what he would have wished should happen to the third son, the old man exclaimed 'Qu'il mourût'; and Boileau comments, 'Voilà de fort petites paroles; cependant il n'y a personne qui ne sente la grandeur héroïque qui est renfermée dans ce mot, *qu'il mourût*, qui est d'autant plus sublime, qu'il est simple et naturel.' Before Boileau, Shakespeare had recognized instinctively that the greater the force of emotion in climactic passages, the simpler should be the vehicle of language. We need only to remember 'the rest is silence', or 'I prithee undo this button'. Wordsworth shows the same understanding. If at times we must convict him of achieving the bathos, on many more occasions he reaches the true sublime, and perhaps nowhere so impressively as in 'Michael'. At the climax of the penultimate paragraph (p. 133), he wrote a line ('And never lifted up a single stone') of which it is perfectly appropriate to echo Boileau and say: Voilà de fort petites paroles; cependant il n'y a personne qui ne sente la grandeur.'

He is equally capable of the majestic and the simple; and it would be difficult to decide which is the more characteristic. But a mannerism of his lofty style deserves consideration. He seems often to forget about his doctrines of the language of conversation, and to pick for the position in his paragraph that is to carry the greatest weight, not a simple word, but some grand Latin polysyllable; and often it is not of a positive but a negative formation, as though to suggest something beyond man's power to reckon. Thus when in *The Prelude*, Book I, he wrestles to describe the indescribable, as the forces of Nature work their way upon him (p. 44), he says that he

> heard among the solitary hills
> Low breathings coming after me, and sounds
> Of *undistinguishable* motion.   (ll. 322–4)

The same apparent resistance to certain knowledge is found a
little later when he exclaims:

> Dust as we are, the immortal spirit grows
> Like harmony in music; there is a dark
> *Inscrutable* workmanship that reconciles
> Discordant elements.   (ll. 340–3)

The antique grandeur of the four yew-trees of Borrowdale is
similarly described (p. 178); the fibres of the 'fraternal four'
are '*inveterately* convolved'; and when in the sonnet on
'Mutability' (p. 207) he uses the image of Time splitting the
tower of a ruined building, he has recourse to the same
device to convey the inscrutable nature of the action.

Lastly, the conclusion of the 'Toussaint L'Ouverture'
sonnet (p. 158) shows not only this mannerism once again, and
the abandoment of the simple for the lofty as he soars to his
conclusion, but it also illustrates the union of themes underlying his best work: the mind of man the main region of his
song and, allied to that theme, the forces of nature and the
mutual sympathy of men in society:

> Live, and take comfort. Thou hast left behind
> Powers that will work for thee; air, earth, and skies;
> There's not a breathing of the common wind
> That will forget thee; thou hast great allies;
> Thy friends are exultations, agonies,
> And love, and man's *unconquerable* mind.

V

Wordsworth was not a poet neglected by contemporary
critics. The three principal journals of the day published re-
views of his first poems, *An Evening Walk* and *Descriptive
Sketches* (1793), and *Lyrical Ballads* received even wider attention. It is sometimes said that *Lyrical Ballads* was so unusual

in kind that readers were mystified and resentful; but except for Southey's notice in *The Critical Review*, none of the reviewers was noticeably hostile. Magazine readers of the day were accustomed to ballads on pastoral life, meditations on nature, reflections induced by the sentiment of place, and tales of suffering rustics; and at a time when the laws of copyright were not so strict as they are today, magazine editors seem to have been delighted to discover in the volume a new quarry to be worked: judging by the number of magazine reprints, 'Goody Blake and Harry Gill' seems to have been especially popular. It was Coleridge's opinion (expressed in *Biographia Literaria*, ch. iv) that 'the true origin of the unexampled opposition which Mr. Wordsworth's writings have been since doomed to encounter' rested in the prose prefaces. The theories were objectionable, perhaps even politically objectionable, and the poems when re-read were discovered to exemplify the theories. Thus the *Edinburgh Review*, entering upon its long and bitter feud with Wordsworth in a review of Southey's poem *Thalaba* (1802), began by taking offence at his theory of diction, and then discovered that 'the depravation of language' extended to the sentiments and emotions expressed: 'a splenetic and idle discontent with the existing institutions of society, seems to be at the bottom of all [his] serious and peculiar sentiments . . . for all sorts of vice and profligacy in the lower orders of society, [he has] the same virtuous horror, and the same tender compassion.'

The Edinburgh Reviewers were later to abandon the political objection, and charged Wordsworth instead with 'silliness', 'puerility', 'affectation', 'childishness', 'insipidity', 'mysticism', and 'prolixity'. Yet they could not leave him alone. Jeffrey, the editor, had to admit that *Lyrical Ballads* were deservedly popular owing to their 'strong spirit of originality, of pathos, and of natural feeling'; and even in the

notorious review of *The Excursion*, which began, 'This will
never do', he devoted almost as many pages to commend-
ing the force of Wordsworth's moral declamations and the
'tenderness in his pathetic narratives' as he gave to ridiculing
his failings.

   But Wordsworth had other critics endowed with greater
sympathy and perception—Hazlitt, Lamb, De Quincey, and
Coleridge above all, by virtue of his critical pre-eminence and
of the length and intimacy of his association with Wordsworth. Fond of each other as he and Wordsworth were, and
influential as each was upon the other's intellectual, spiritual,
and artistic development, they were by no means identical
in their outlook. They were close enough to try poetical
collaboration, but they soon abandoned the attempt; and the
division of labour in *Lyrical Ballads* suggests that they already
recognized that their interests were at best complementary,
perhaps even antithetical. Their views on the relationship of
man and nature were to diverge as the years went by; and
Coleridge, who was certainly responsible for releasing
Wordsworth's power of meditating on his own mind, was
to lament in his latter days that Wordsworth had failed to
write the philosophical poem whose outlines Coleridge had
drawn for him.

   Some regret at what was unfinished in Wordsworth's mind
and art—at what perhaps he felt that he himself had left unfinished in them—is apparent in Coleridge's criticism of his
friend's work in *Biographia Literaria* (1817). Thus he was at
pains to point out the logical objections to Wordsworth's
theory of diction, but was less careful to explain what Wordsworth can be supposed to have meant. In a subsequent
chapter (xxii) he examined the 'characteristic defects' and
beauties of Wordsworth's poetry. Amongst the defects he
noticed an occasional 'inconsistency of style . . . the sudden

and unprepared transitions from lines or sentences of peculiar felicity . . . to a style, not only unimpassioned but undistinguished', an incongruity which he proceeded to illustrate from 'Resolution and Independence'. Wordsworth took notice of the objection, and revised the poem accordingly (see p. 228). The second defect he discovered was 'a laborious minuteness and fidelity in the representation of objects' and 'the insertion of accidental circumstances, in order to the full explanation of his living characters'. This also was a defect that Wordsworth was at pains to avoid, as he showed in his revision of 'Animal Tranquillity and Decay' (p. 221) and several passages of *The Prelude* (e.g. p. 218).

Coleridge listed three other defects, 'an undue predilection for the dramatic form', 'occasional prolixity', and 'a disproportion of thought to the circumstance and occasion', shown notably, so Coleridge considered, in Wordsworth's addressing 'the six years' darling' of the 'Immortality' Ode as 'Mighty Prophet! Seer blest!'

Yet how small were these defects in proportion to the beauties, 'the austere purity of language', the 'weight and sanity of the Thoughts and Sentiments, won . . . from the poet's own meditative observation', 'the sinewy strength and originality of single lines and paragraphs', 'the perfect truth of nature in his images and descriptions', and, pre-eminently, 'the gift of imagination in the highest and strictest sense of the word'.

In imaginative power Coleridge placed his friend nearest to Shakespeare and Milton, and in other respects with Goethe. This concern for the poet's standing is the mark of Matthew Arnold's criticism of Wordsworth from the time of his 'Memorial Verses' on the poet's death to his introductory essay to the 'Golden Treasury' selection from Wordsworth's poems published twenty-nine years later. From this time onwards Wordsworth was felt to stand amongst the very greatest; and for Arnold he had earned this position

because of the extraordinary power with which [he] feels the joy offered to us in nature, the joy offered to us in the simple primary affections and duties; and because of the extraordinary power with which ... he shows us this joy, and renders it so as to make us share it.

If critics today pay less attention to this 'joy' than Arnold did, it is not that they do not feel the joy (or so at least we must hope) as that they have become fascinated with other aspects of Wordsworth's work. The emphasis of modern criticism of Wordsworth has long been fundamentally biographical: the nature of his mystical experience, the relationship of that experience to his expression of it, and the explanation of his fading powers. There is no sign yet that this interest is exhausted, and no reason to fear that readers will cease to feel challenged by his genius.

VI

The arrangement of the poems has presented a difficult problem. To have attempted a strictly chronological order of composition or of publication could only have caused misunderstanding, for some of Wordsworth's poems were written over a period of several years, and many were revised in important particulars after their first appearance in print. Thus the writing of *The Prelude* occupied seven years and the writing of *The Excursion* nineteen. They were both revised, and so were many of the shorter poems; thus the versions of 'Resolution and Independence' and the 'Immortality' Ode that we read today differ appreciably from the versions that first appeared in 1807, and the revised version of 'Simon Lee' printed on page 88 might have given less offence to first readers than the version printed in *Lyrical Ballads*.

Wordsworth himself preferred an arrangement based on the subject treated, such as 'Poems referring to the period of childhood', or on the powers of mind predominant in the composition, such as 'Poems of the Imagination'. This is an arrangement that has given little satisfaction; but at least it serves to emphasize some important similarities in theme that might be overlooked in an order based on chronology. In this selection it has been decided to group the great majority of the shorter poems under the titles of the volumes in which they first appeared, and thus to represent the quality of Wordsworth's three principal collections, *Lyrical Ballads*, 1798, *Lyrical Ballads*, volume ii, 1800, and *Poems*, 1807; but some liberties have been taken so as to bring together poems that have a natural affinity. The first item is chosen as a 'glad preamble' to the whole book, but more especially to the episodes from *The Prelude* which happen to illustrate its doctrine. After 'The Old Cumberland Beggar' (an early poem), there follows an appendix to it, with other poems first printed in *Lyrical Ballads*. The 'Lucy' poems have been grouped at the end of the selection taken from the second volume of *Lyrical Ballads*, 1800, so as to unite them with the last of the 'Lucy' poems first printed in *Poems*, 1807. It was felt that certain poems selected from that book could be brought together with advantage, for example the three poems inspired by encounters with vagrants, the two groups of sonnets, the two odes, and several others which readers will quickly notice. Five poems published later than 1807 have also been assembled with the 1807 poems in the interest of natural relationship—a second sonnet on the sonnet form, a later sonnet on national independence and liberty, a later Yarrow poem, a later poem inspired by grave personal loss, and an imaginative poem written before 1807 and omitted from those volumes perhaps by accident. Then, following the extracts from *The Excursion*, are seven poems from Words-worth's later years, chosen to represent the moments of inspiration that still sometimes visited him. In every instance the text of the poem is the revised text, and is taken from the standard edition in six volumes edited by Ernest de Selincourt and Helen Darbishire. The text of *The Prelude* is also the revised text, and is taken from the standard edition by the same editors.

CHRONOLOGICAL TABLE

1770 William Wordsworth born at Cockermouth, Cumberland (7 April).

1771 Dorothy Wordsworth born (25 December).

1772 Coleridge born (21 October).

1778 Death of Wordsworth's mother.

1779 Sent to school at Hawkshead.

1783 Death of Wordsworth's father.

1787 Entered St. John's College, Cambridge.

1790 Walking-tour with Robert Jones in France and Switzerland (July–October).

1791 Graduated Bachelor of Arts (27 January).
Visit to France began (28 November).

1792 Birth of Wordsworth's daughter, Anne-Caroline, by Annette Vallon (15 December).
Return to England (December).

1793 *An Evening Walk* and *Descriptive Sketches* published.
Walking tour from London to North Wales, through the Wye valley.

1794 Visits Windy Brow, Keswick, with Dorothy (spring).
Nurses Raisley Calvert at Windy Brow (summer and autumn).

1795 Calvert bequeathed Wordsworth £900 (January).
First meeting with William Godwin, author of *Political Justice* (February).
First meeting with Coleridge at Bristol (August).
At Racedown Lodge, Dorset with Dorothy (26 September).

1796 Coleridge settles at Nether Stowey (31 December).

1797 Wordsworth visits Coleridge (March).
Coleridge visits Wordsworth (June).
Wordsworth moves with Dorothy to Alfoxden House, Somerset, to be nearer Coleridge (July).
Kubla Khan written (October ?).
The Ancient Mariner and *Christabel* begun (November).

1798 *The Ruined Cottage* expanded (March).
The Recluse begun (March).
Peter Bell begun (April).
'Lines Composed . . . above Tintern Abbey' written (July).
Lyrical Ballads published (September).
Coleridge and the Wordsworths sail for Germany (September).
Wordsworth and Dorothy at Goslar (October).
The 'Lucy' poems written; *The Prelude* begun.

1799 The Wordsworths return to England, and to Sockburn-on-Tees, the home of Mary Hutchinson (May).
Walking tour in the Lake District with Coleridge (October and November).
Settled at Dove Cottage, Grasmere, with Dorothy (December).

1801 *Lyrical Ballads*, second edition, published January.

1802 'Ode: Intimations of Immortality' begun (March).
Peace of Amiens (March).
Visit to Calais with Dorothy for settlement with Annette Vallon (August).
Marriage with Mary Hutchinson (October).

1803 Tour of Scotland with Coleridge and Dorothy.
First meeting with Scott.

1805 *The Prelude* completed.
Wordsworth's brother, John, drowned (February).

1807 *Poems in Two Volumes* published.

1808 The Wordsworths move to Allen Bank, Grasmere.

1810 Estrangement from Coleridge.

1812 Reconciliation with Coleridge.

1813 Made Distributor of Stamps for Westmorland.
Move to Rydal Mount, Grasmere.

1814 *The Excursion* published.

1815 *Poems*, first collected edition, published.

1843 Appointed Poet Laureate.
Dictates notes on his poems to Miss Fenwick.

1850 Death of Wordsworth (23 April).
The Prelude published.

SELECT BIBLIOGRAPHY

I. EDITIONS OF WORDSWORTH'S WORKS

(a) Collected Works

The Poetical Works, 5 vols. (London, 1827); 4 vols. (London, 1832); 6 vols. (London, 1836–7); 7 vols. (London, 1842); 6 vols. (London, 1849–50).

The Poetical Works, ed. E. de Selincourt and Helen Darbishire. 5 vols. (Oxford, 1940–9).
  The standard edition.

The Letters of William and Dorothy Wordsworth, 1787–1850, ed. E. de Selincourt. 6 vols. (Oxford, 1935–9).
  There is a selection in the World's Classics series.

(b) Selections and Separate Works

An Evening Walk (London, 1793).

Descriptive Sketches (London, 1793).

Lyrical Ballads (Bristol and London, 1798).

Lyrical Ballads, with other poems. 2 vols. (London, 1800).
  Contains the famous critical preface; revised in subsequent editions, 1802, 1805.

Poems in Two Volumes (London, 1807).

The Excursion, being a portion of The Recluse, a poem (London, 1814).

Poems. 2 vols. (London, 1815).
  Contains an important preface.

The White Doe of Rylstone (London, 1815).

Peter Bell (London, 1819).
  Written 1798.

The Waggoner (London, 1819).

The River Duddon, a series of sonnets (London, 1820).

Ecclesiastical Sketches (London, 1822).
  The title was changed to *Ecclesiastical Sonnets* in 1837.

Yarrow Revisited, and other poems (London, 1835).

Poems, chiefly of early and late years; including The Borderers, a tragedy (London, 1842).

The Prelude, or Growth of a Poet's Mind (London, 1850).
>   This is a revised version. The original version of 1805 was first published by E. de Selincourt (Oxford, 1926); second edition, revised by Helen Darbishire (Oxford, 1959).

The Recluse (London, 1888).

(*c*) *Prose*

[See above, under *Lyrical Ballads*, 1800, and *Poems*, 1815]

Concerning the relations of Great Britain, Spain and Portugal . . . as affected by the Convention of Cintra (London, 1809).

A Description of the Scenery of the Lakes in the North of England (London, 1822).
>   The first separate edition. It had first appeared in 1810. Its more familiar title, *A Guide through the District of the Lakes in the North of England*, was first used in the edition of 1835. Ed. E. de Selincourt, 1906; ed. W. M. Merchant, 1951.

II. BIOGRAPHY AND CRITICISM

S. T. Coleridge, *Biographia Literaria* (London, 1817); ed. J. Shawcross, 2 vols. (London, 1907).
>   See particularly chapters 4, 14, 17–22.

E. Legouis, *The Early Life of William Wordsworth* (London, 1897).

W. Raleigh, *Wordsworth* (London, 1903).

G. M. Harper, *William Wordsworth, his life, works, and influence.* 2 vols. (London, 1916).

H. W. Garrod, *Wordsworth* (Oxford, 1923).

Dorothy Wordsworth, *Journals*, ed. E. de Selincourt, 2 vols. (London, 1942).
>   First published in 1897, ed W. Knight; there is a complete text of the *Grasmere Journal*, ed. Helen Darbishire, in the World's Classics series (London, 1958).

J. C. Smith, *A Study of Wordsworth* (Edinburgh and London, 1944).

Helen Darbishire, *The Poet Wordsworth* (Oxford, 1950).

L. Abercrombie, *The Art of Wordsworth* (London, 1952).

H. M. Margoliouth, *Wordsworth and Coleridge 1795–1834* (London, 1953).

J. Jones, *The Egotistical Sublime: a history of Wordsworth's imagination* (London, 1954).

Mary Moorman, *William Wordsworth, a biography: the early years, 1770–1803* (Oxford, 1957).

Mary Moorman, *William Wordsworth, a biography: the later years, 1803–1850* (Oxford, 1965).

FROM THE RECLUSE

'Prospectus'

Written 1798. Published, *The Excursion* (1814)

ON Man, on Nature, and on Human Life,
Musing in solitude, I oft perceive
Fair trains of imagery before me rise,
Accompanied by feelings of delight
Pure, or with no unpleasing sadness mixed;   5
And I am conscious of affecting thoughts
And dear remembrances, whose presence soothes
Or elevates the Mind, intent to weigh
The good and evil of our mortal state.
—To these emotions, whencesoe'er they come,   10
Whether from breath of outward circumstance,
Or from the Soul—an impulse to herself—
I would give utterance in numerous verse.
Of Truth, of Grandeur, Beauty, Love, and Hope,
And melancholy Fear subdued by Faith;   15
Of blessèd consolations in distress;
Of moral strength, and intellectual Power;
Of joy in widest commonalty spread;
Of the individual Mind that keeps her own
Inviolate retirement, subject there   20
To Conscience only, and the law supreme
Of that Intelligence which governs all—
I sing:—'fit audience let me find though few!'

So prayed, more gaining then he asked, the Bard—
In holiest mood. Urania, I shall need   25
Thy guidance, or a greater Muse, if such
Descend to earth or dwell in highest heaven!
For I must tread on shadowy ground, must sink
Deep—and, aloft ascending, breathe in worlds
To which the heaven of heavens is but a veil.   30
All strength—all terror, single or in bands,
That ever was put forth in personal form—
Jehovah—with his thunder, and the choir
Of shouting Angels, and the empyreal thrones—
I pass them unalarmed. Not Chaos, not   35
The darkest pit of lowest Erebus,
Nor aught of blinder vacancy, scooped out
By help of dreams—can breed such fear and awe
As fall upon us often when we look
Into our Minds, into the Mind of Man—   40
My haunt, and the main region of my song.
—Beauty—a living Presence of the earth,
Surpassing the most fair ideal Forms
Which craft of delicate Spirits hath composed
From earth's materials—waits upon my steps;   45
Pitches her tents before me as I move,
An hourly neighbour. Paradise, and groves
Elysian, Fortunate Fields—like those of old
Sought in the Atlantic Main—why should they be
A history only of departed things,   50
Or a mere fiction of what never was?
For the discerning intellect of Man,
When wedded to this goodly universe
In love and holy passion, shall find these
A simple produce of the common day.   55
—I, long before the blissful hour arrives,

Would chant, in lonely peace, the spousal verse
Of this great consummation:—and, by words
Which speak of nothing more than what we are,
Would I arouse the sensual from their sleep   60
Of Death, and win the vacant and the vain
To noble raptures; while my voice proclaims
How exquisitely the individual Mind
(And the progressive powers perhaps no less
Of the whole species) to the external World   65
Is fitted:—and how exquisitely, too—
Theme this but little heard of among men—
The external World is fitted to the Mind;
And the creation (by no lower name
Can it be called) which they with blended might   70
Accomplish:—this is our high argument.
—Such grateful haunts foregoing, if I oft
Must turn elsewhere—to travel near the tribes
And fellowships of men, and see ill sights
Of madding passions mutually inflamed;   75
Must hear Humanity in fields and groves
Pipe solitary anguish; or must hang
Brooding above the fierce confederate storm
Of sorrow, barricadoed evermore
Within the walls of cities—may these sounds   80
Have their authentic comment; that even these
Hearing, I be not downcast or forlorn!—
Descend, prophetic Spirit! that inspir'st
The human Soul of universal earth,
Dreaming on things to come; and dost possess   85
A metropolitan temple in the hearts
Of mighty Poets: upon me bestow
A gift of genuine insight; that my Song
With star-like virtue in its place may shine,

Shedding benignant influence, and secure,   90
Itself, from all malevolent effect
Of those mutations that extend their sway
Throughout the nether sphere!—And if with this
I mix more lowly matter; with the thing
Contemplated, describe the Mind and Man   95
Contemplating; and who, and what he was—
The transitory Being that beheld
This Vision; when and where, and how he lived;—
Be not this labour useless. If such theme
May sort with highest objects, then—dread Power!   100
Whose gracious favour is the primal source
Of all illumination,—may my Life
Express the image of a better time,
More wise desires, and simpler manners;—nurse
My Heart in genuine freedom:—all pure thoughts   105
Be with me;—so shall thy unfailing love
Guide, and support, and cheer me to the end!

FROM THE PRELUDE

PUBLISHED 1850

Book I. Childhood and School-time

Written 1798-9

FAIR seed-time had my soul, and I grew up
Fostered alike by beauty and by fear:
Much favoured in my birth-place, and no less
In that beloved Vale to which erelong
We were transplanted—there were we let loose   305
For sports of wider range. Ere I had told
Ten birth-days, when among the mountain slopes
Frost, and the breath of frosty wind, had snapped
The last autumnal crocus, 'twas my joy
With store of springes o'er my shoulder hung   310
To range the open heights where woodcocks run
Along the smooth green turf. Through half the night,
Scudding away from snare to snare, I plied
That anxious visitation;—moon and stars
Were shining o'er my head. I was alone,   315
And seemed to be a trouble to the peace
That dwelt among them. Sometimes it befel
In these night wanderings, that a strong desire
O'erpowered my better reason, and the bird
Which was the captive of another's toil   320
Became my prey; and when the deed was done

I heard among the solitary hills
Low breathings coming after me, and sounds
Of undistinguishable motion, steps
Almost as silent as the turf they trod.   325
   Nor less when spring had warmed the cultured Vale,
Moved we as plunderers where the mother-bird
Had in high places built her lodge; though mean
Our object and inglorious, yet the end
Was not ignoble. Oh! when I have hung   330
Above the raven's nest, by knots of grass
And half-inch fissures in the slippery rock
But ill sustained, and almost (so it seemed)
Suspended by the blast that blew amain,
Shouldering the naked crag, oh, at that time   335
While on the perilous ridge I hung alone,
With what strange utterance did the loud dry wind
Blow through my ear! the sky seemed not a sky
Of earth—and with what motion moved the clouds!
   Dust as we are, the immortal spirit grows   340
Like harmony in music; there is a dark
Inscrutable workmanship that reconciles
Discordant elements, makes them cling together
In one society. How strange that all
The terrors, pains, and early miseries,   345
Regrets, vexations, lassitudes interfused
Within my mind, should e'er have borne a part,
And that a needful part, in making up
The calm existence that is mine when I
Am worthy of myself! Praise to the end!   350
Thanks to the means which Nature deigned to employ;
Whether her fearless visitings, or those
That came with soft alarm, like hurtless light
Opening the peaceful clouds; or she may use

Severer interventions, ministry   355
  More palpable, as best might suit her aim.
    One summer evening (led by her) I found
A little boat tied to a willow tree
Within a rocky cave, its usual home.
Straight I unloosed her chain, and stepping in   360
Pushed from the shore. It was an act of stealth
And troubled pleasure, nor without the voice
Of mountain-echoes did my boat move on;
Leaving behind her still, on either side,
Small circles glittering idly in the moon,   365
Until they melted all into one track
Of sparkling light. But now, like one who rows,
Proud of his skill, to reach a chosen point
With an unswerving line, I fixed my view
Upon the summit of a craggy ridge,   370
The horizon's utmost boundary; far above
Was nothing but the stars and the grey sky.
She was an elfin pinnace; lustily
I dipped my oars into the silent lake,
And, as I rose upon the stroke, my boat   375
Went heaving through the water like a swan;
When, from behind that craggy steep till then
The horizon's bound, a huge peak, black and huge,
As if with voluntary power instinct
Upreared its head. I struck and struck again,   380
And growing still in stature the grim shape
Towered up between me and the stars, and still,
For so it seemed, with purpose of its own
And measured motion like a living thing,
Strode after me. With trembling oars I turned,   385
And through the silent water stole my way
Back to the covert of the willow tree;

There in her mooring-place I left my bark,—
And through the meadows homeward went, in grave
And serious mood; but after I had seen   390
That spectacle, for many days, my brain
Worked with a dim and undetermined sense
Of unknown modes of being; o'er my thoughts
There hung a darkness, call it solitude
Or blank desertion. No familiar shapes   395
Remained, no pleasant images of trees,
Of sea or sky, no colours of green fields;
But huge and mighty forms, that do not live
Like living men, moved slowly through the mind
By day, and were a trouble to my dreams.   400
  Wisdom and Spirit of the universe!
Thou Soul that art the eternity of thought,
That givest to forms and images a breath
And everlasting motion, not in vain
By day or star-light thus from my first dawn   405
Of childhood didst thou intertwine for me
The passions that build up our human soul;
Not with the mean and vulgar works of man,
But with high objects, with enduring things—
With life and nature, purifying thus   410
The elements of feeling and of thought,
And sanctifying, by such discipline,
Both pain and fear, until we recognise
A grandeur in the beatings of the heart. . . .
  And in the frosty season, when the sun   425
Was set, and visible for many a mile
The cottage windows blazed through twilight gloom,
I heeded not their summons: happy time
It was indeed for all of us—for me
It was a time of rapture! Clear and loud   430

The village clock tolled six,—I wheeled about,
Proud and exulting like an untired horse
That cares not for his home. All shod with steel,
We hissed along the polished ice in games
Confederate, imitative of the chase   435
And woodland pleasures,—the resounding horn,
The pack loud chiming, and the hunted hare.
So through the darkness and the cold we flew,
And not a voice was idle; with the din
Smitten, the precipices rang aloud;   440
The leafless trees and every icy crag
Tinkled like iron; while far distant hills
Into the tumult sent an alien sound
Of melancholy not unnoticed, while the stars
Eastward were sparkling clear, and in the west   445
The orange sky of evening died away.
Not seldom from the uproar I retired
Into a silent bay, or sportively
Glanced sideway, leaving the tumultuous throng,
To cut across the reflex of a star   450
That fled, and, flying still before me, gleamed
Upon the glassy plain; and oftentimes,
When we had given our bodies to the wind,
And all the shadowy banks on either side
Came sweeping through the darkness, spinning still   455
The rapid line of motion, then at once
Have I, reclining back upon my heels,
Stopped short; yet still the solitary cliffs
Wheeled by me—even as if the earth had rolled
With visible motion her diurnal round!   460
Behind me did they stretch in solemn train,
Feebler and feebler, and I stood and watched
Till all was tranquil as a dreamless sleep.

Ye Presences of Nature in the sky
And on the earth! Ye Visions of the hills!   465
And Souls of lonely places! can I think
A vulgar hope was yours when ye employed
Such ministry, when ye through many a year
Haunting me thus among my boyish sports,
On caves and trees, upon the woods and hills,   470
Impressed upon all forms the characters
Of danger or desire; and thus did make
The surface of the universal earth
With triumph and delight, with hope and fear,
Work like a sea?   475
              Not uselessly employed,
Might I pursue this theme through every change
Of exercise and play, to which the year
Did summon us in his delightful round.

We were a noisy crew; the sun in heaven
Beheld not vales more beautiful than ours;   480
Nor saw a band in happiness and joy
Richer, or worthier of the ground they trod.
I could record with no reluctant voice
The woods of autumn, and their hazel bowers
With milk-white clusters hung; the rod and line,   485
True symbol of hope's foolishness, whose strong
And unreproved enchantment led us on
By rocks and pools shut out from every star,
All the green summer, to forlorn cascades
Among the windings hid of mountain brook   490
—Unfading recollections! at this hour
The heart is almost mine with which I felt,
From some hill-top on sunny afternoons,
The paper kite high among fleecy clouds
Pull at her rein like an impetuous courser;   495

Or, from the meadows sent on gusty days,
Beheld her breast the wind, then suddenly
Dashed headlong, and rejected by the storm.
    Ye lowly cottages wherein we dwelt,
A ministration of your own was yours;   500
Can I forget you, being as you were
So beautiful among the pleasant fields
In which ye stood? or can I here forget
The plain and seemly countenance with which
Ye dealt out your plain comforts? Yet had ye   505
Delights and exultations of your own.
Eager and never weary we pursued
Our home-amusements by the warm peat-fire
At evening, when with pencil, and smooth slate
In square divisions parcelled out and all   510
With crosses and with cyphers scribbled o'er,
We schemed and puzzled, head opposed to head
In strife too humble to be named in verse:
Or round the naked table, snow-white deal,
Cherry or maple, sate in close array,   515
And to the combat, Loo or Whist, led on
A thick-ribbed army; not, as in the world,
Neglected and ungratefully thrown by
Even for the very service they had wrought,
But husbanded through many a long campaign.   520
Uncouth assemblage was it, where no few
Had changed their functions; some, plebeian cards
Which Fate, beyond the promise of their birth,
Had dignified, and called to represent
The persons of departed potentates.   525
Oh, with what echoes on the board they fell!
Ironic diamonds,—clubs, hearts, diamonds, spades,
A congregation piteously akin!

Cheap matter offered they to boyish wit,
Those sooty knaves, precipitated down   530
With scoffs and taunts, like Vulcan out of heaven:
The paramount ace, a moon in her eclipse,
Queens gleaming through their splendour's last decay,
And monarchs surly at the wrongs sustained
By royal visages. Meanwhile abroad   535
Incessant rain was falling, or the frost
Raged bitterly, with keen and silent tooth;
And, interrupting oft that eager game,
From under Esthwaite's splitting fields of ice
The pent-up air, struggling to free itself,   540
Gave out to meadow grounds and hills a loud
Protracted yelling, like the noise of wolves
Howling in troops along the Bothnic Main.

   Nor, sedulous as I have been to trace
How Nature by extrinsic passion first   545
Peopled the mind with forms sublime or fair,
And made me love them, may I here omit
How other pleasures have been mine, and joys
Of subtler origin; how I have felt,
Not seldom even in that tempestuous time,   550
Those hallowed and pure motions of the sense
Which seem, in their simplicity, to own
An intellectual charm; that calm delight
Which, if I err not, surely must belong
To those first-born affinities that fit   555
Our new existence to existing things,
And, in our dawn of being, constitute
The bond of union between life and joy. . . .

Book II. School-time

Written 1800

OUR daily meals were frugal, Sabine fare!
More than we wished we knew the blessing then
Of vigorous hunger—hence corporeal strength   80
Unsapped by delicate viands; for, exclude
A little weekly stipend, and we lived
Through three divisions of the quartered year
In penniless poverty. But now to school
From the half-yearly holidays returned,   85
We came with weightier purses, that sufficed
To furnish treats more costly than the Dame
Of the old grey stone, from her scant board, supplied.
Hence rustic dinners on the cool green ground,
Or in the woods, or by a river side   90
Or shady fountains, while among the leaves
Soft airs were stirring, and the mid-day sun
Unfelt shone brightly round us in our joy.
Nor is my aim neglected if I tell
How sometimes, in the length of those half-years,   95
We from our funds drew largely;—proud to curb,
And eager to spur on, the galloping steed;
And with the courteous inn-keeper, whose stud
Supplied our want, we haply might employ
Sly subterfuge, if the adventure's bound   100
Were distant: some famed temple where of yore
The Druids worshipped, or the antique walls
Of that large abbey, where within the Vale
Of Nightshade, to St. Mary's honour built,
Stands yet a mouldering pile with fractured arch,   105
Belfry, and images, and living trees,

A holy scene! Along the smooth green turf
Our horses grazed. To more than inland peace
Left by the west wind sweeping overhead
From a tumultuous ocean, trees and towers   110
In that sequestered valley may be seen,
Both silent and both motionless alike;
Such the deep shelter that is there, and such
The safeguard for repose and quietness.

   Our steeds remounted and the summons given,   115
With whip and spur we through the chauntry flew
In uncouth race, and left the cross-legged knight,
And the stone-abbot, and that single wren
Which one day sang so sweetly in the nave
Of the old church, that—though from recent showers 120
The earth was comfortless, and touched by faint
Internal breezes, sobbings of the place
And respirations, from the roofless walls
The shuddering ivy dripped large drops—yet still
So sweetly 'mid the gloom the invisible bird   125
Sang to herself, that there I could have made
My dwelling-place, and lived for ever there
To hear such music. Through the walls we flew
And down the valley, and, a circuit made
In wantonness of heart, through rough and smooth   130
We scampered homewards. Oh, ye rocks and streams,
And that still spirit shed from evening air!
Even in this joyous time I sometimes felt
Your presence, when with slackened step we breathed
Along the sides of the steep hills, or when   135
Lighted by gleams of moonlight from the sea
We beat with thundering hoofs the level sand. . . .
                   'Twere long to tell   352
What spring and autumn, what the winter snows,

And what the summer shade, what day and night,
Evening and morning, sleep and waking, thought   355
From sources inexhaustible, poured forth
To feed the spirit of religious love
In which I walked with Nature. But let this
Be not forgotten, that I still retained
My first creative sensibility;   360
That by the regular action of the world
My soul was unsubdued. A plastic power
Abode with me; a forming hand, at times
Rebellious, acting in a devious mood;
A local spirit of his own, at war   365
With general tendency, but, for the most,
Subservient strictly to external things
With which it communed. An auxiliar light
Came from my mind, which on the setting sun
Bestowed new splendour; the melodious birds,   370
The fluttering breezes, fountains that run on
Murmuring so sweetly in themselves, obeyed
A like dominion, and the midnight storm
Grew darker in the presence of my eye:
Hence my obeisance, my devotion hence,   375
And hence my transport.
                       Nor should this, perchance,
Pass unrecorded, that I still had loved
The exercise and produce of a toil,
Than analytic industry to me
More pleasing, and whose character I deem   380
Is more poetic as resembling more
Creative agency. The song would speak
Of that interminable building reared
By observation of affinities
In objects where no brotherhood exists   385

To passive minds. My seventeenth year was come;
And, whether from this habit rooted now
So deeply in my mind, or from excess
In the great social principle of life
Coercing all things into sympathy,   390
To unorganic natures were transferred
My own enjoyments; or the power of truth
Coming in revelation, did converse
With things that really are; I, at this time,
Saw blessings spread around me like a sea.   395
Thus while the days flew by, and years passed on,
From Nature and her overflowing soul,
I had received so much, that all my thoughts
Were steeped in feeling; I was only then
Contented, when with bliss ineffable   400
I felt the sentiment of Being spread
O'er all that moves and all that seemeth still;
O'er all that, lost beyond the reach of thought
And human knowledge, to the human eye
Invisible, yet liveth to the heart;   405
O'er all that leaps and runs, and shouts and sings,
Or beats the gladsome air; o'er all that glides
Beneath the wave, yea, in the wave itself,
And mighty depth of waters. Wonder not
If high the transport, great the joy I felt,   410
Communing in this sort through earth and heaven
With every form of creature, as it looked
Towards the Uncreated with a countenance
Of adoration, with an eye of love.
One song they sang, and it was audible,   415
Most audible, then, when the fleshly ear,
O'ercome by humblest prelude of that strain,
Forgot her functions, and slept undisturbed.

If this be error, and another faith
Find easier access to the pious mind, 420
Yet were I grossly destitute of all
Those human sentiments that make this earth
So dear, if I should fail with grateful voice
To speak of you, ye mountains, and ye lakes
And sounding cataracts, ye mists and winds 425
That dwell among the hills where I was born.
If in my youth I have been pure in heart,
If, mingling with the world, I am content
With my own modest pleasures, and have lived
With God and Nature communing, removed 430
From little enmities and low desires,
The gift is yours; if in these times of fear,
This melancholy waste of hopes o'erthrown,
If, 'mid indifference and apathy,
And wicked exultation when good men 435
On every side fall off, we know not how,
To selfishness, disguised in gentle names
Of peace and quiet and domestic love,
Yet mingled not unwillingly with sneers
On visionary minds; if, in this time 440
Of dereliction and dismay, I yet
Despair not of our nature, but retain
A more than Roman confidence, a faith
That fails not, in all sorrow my support,
The blessing of my life; the gift is yours, 445
Ye winds and sounding cataracts! 'tis yours,
Ye mountains! thine, O Nature! Thou hast fed
My lofty speculations; and in thee,
For this uneasy heart of ours, I find
A never-failing principle of joy 450
And purest passion. . . .

Book III. Residence at Cambridge

Written 1801

It was a dreary morning when the wheels
Rolled over a wide plain o'erhung with clouds,
And nothing cheered our way till first we saw
The long-roofed chapel of King's College lift
Turrets and pinnacles in answering files,   5
Extended high above a dusky grove.
   Advancing, we espied upon the road
A student clothed in gown and tasselled cap,
Striding along as if o'ertasked by Time,
Or covetous of exercise and air;   10
He passed—nor was I master of my eyes
Till he was left an arrow's flight behind.
As near and nearer to the spot we drew,
It seemed to suck us in with an eddy's force.
Onward we drove beneath the Castle; caught,   15
While crossing Magdalene Bridge, a glimpse of Cam;
And at the *Hoop* alighted, famous Inn.
   My spirit was up, my thoughts were full of hope;
Some friends I had, acquaintances who there
Seemed friends, poor simple school-boys, now hung round 20
With honour and importance: in a world
Of welcome faces up and down I roved;
Questions, directions, warnings and advice,
Flowed in upon me, from all sides; fresh day
Of pride and pleasure! to myself I seemed   25
A man of business and expense, and went
From shop to shop about my own affairs,
To Tutor or to Tailor, as befel,

From street to street with loose and careless mind.
　　I was the Dreamer, they the Dream; I roamed   30
Delighted through the motley spectacle;
Gowns grave, or gaudy, doctors, students, streets,
Courts, cloisters, flocks of churches, gateways, towers:
Migration strange for a stripling of the hills,
A northern villager.
　　　　　　　　As if the change   35
Had waited on some Fairy's wand, at once
Behold me rich in monies, and attired
In splendid garb, with hose of silk, and hair
Powdered like rimy trees, when frost is keen.
My lordly dressing-gown, I pass it by,   40
With other signs of manhood that supplied
The lack of beard.—The weeks went roundly on,
With invitations, suppers, wine and fruit,
Smooth housekeeping within, and all without
Liberal, and suiting gentleman's array.   45
　　The Evangelist St. John my patron was:
Three Gothic courts are his, and in the first
Was my abiding-place, a nook obscure;
Right underneath, the College kitchens made
A humming sound, less tuneable than bees,   50
But hardly less industrious; with shrill notes
Of sharp command and scolding intermixed.
Near me hung Trinity's loquacious clock,
Who never let the quarters, night or day,
Slip by him unproclaimed, and told the hours   55
Twice over with a male and female voice.
Her pealing organ was my neighbour too;
And from my pillow, looking forth by light
Of moon or favouring stars, I could behold
The antechapel where the statue stood   60

Of Newton with his prism and silent face,
The marble index of a mind for ever
Voyaging through strange seas of Thought, alone. . . .

Book IV. Summer Vacation

Written 1804

'MID a throng
Of maids and youths, old men, and matrons staid,   310
A medley of all tempers, I had passed
The night in dancing, gaiety, and mirth,
With din of instruments and shuffling feet,
And glancing forms, and tapers glittering,
And unaimed prattle flying up and down;   315
Spirits upon the stretch, and here and there
Slight shocks of young love-liking interspersed,
Whose transient pleasure mounted to the head,
And tingled through the veins. Ere we retired,
The cock had crowed, and now the eastern sky   320
Was kindling, not unseen, from humble copse
And open field, through which the pathway wound,
And homeward led my steps. Magnificent
The morning rose, in memorable pomp,
Glorious as e'er I had beheld—in front,   325
The sea lay laughing at a distance; near,
The solid mountains shone, bright as the clouds,
Grain-tinctured, drenched in empyrean light;
And in the meadows and the lower grounds
Was all the sweetness of a common dawn—   330
Dews, vapours, and the melody of birds,
And labourers going forth to till the fields.

Ah! need I say, dear Friend! that to the brim
My heart was full; I made no vows, but vows
Were then made for me; bond unknown to me   335
Was given, that I should be, else sinning greatly,
A dedicated Spirit. On I walked
In thankful blessedness, which yet survives. . . .

       Once, when those summer months   370
Were flown, and autumn brought its annual show
Of oars with oars contending, sails with sails,
Upon Winander's spacious breast, it chanced
That—after I had left a flower-decked room
(Whose in-door pastime, lighted up, survived   375
To a late hour), and spirits overwrought
Were making night do penance for a day
Spent in a round of strenuous idleness—
My homeward course led up a long ascent,
Where the road's watery surface, to the top   380
Of that sharp rising, glittered to the moon
And bore the semblance of another stream
Stealing with silent lapse to join the brook
That murmured in the vale. All else was still;
No living thing appeared in earth or air,   385
And, save the flowing water's peaceful voice,
Sound there was none—but, lo! an uncouth shape,
Shown by a sudden turning of the road,
So near that, slipping back into the shade
Of a thick hawthorn, I could mark him well,   390
Myself unseen. He was of stature tall,
A span above man's common measure, tall,
Stiff, lank, and upright; a more meagre man
Was never seen before by night or day.
Long were his arms, pallid his hands; his mouth   395
Looked ghastly in the moonlight: from behind,

A mile-stone propped him; I could also ken
That he was clothed in military garb,
Though faded, yet entire. Companionless,
No dog attending, by no staff sustained,   400
He stood, and in his very dress appeared
A desolation, a simplicity,
To which the trappings of a gaudy world
Make a strange back-ground. From his lips, ere long,
Issued low muttered sounds, as if of pain   405
Or some uneasy thought; yet still his form
Kept the same awful steadiness—at his feet
His shadow lay, and moved not. From self-blame
Not wholly free, I watched him thus; at length
Subduing my heart's specious cowardice,   410
I left the shady nook where I had stood
And hailed him. Slowly from his resting-place
He rose, and with a lean and wasted arm
In measured gesture lifted to his head
Returned my salutation; then resumed   415
His station as before; and when I asked
His history, the veteran, in reply,
Was neither slow nor eager; but, unmoved,
And with a quiet uncomplaining voice,
A stately air of mild indifference,   420
He told in few plain words a soldier's tale—
That in the Tropic Islands he had served,
Whence he had landed scarcely three weeks past;
That on his landing he had been dismissed,
And now was travelling towards his native home.   425
This heard, I said, in pity, 'Come with me.'
He stooped, and straightway from the ground took up
An oaken staff by me yet unobserved—
A staff which must have dropt from his slack hand

And lay till now neglected in the grass. 430
Though weak his step and cautious, he appeared
To travel without pain, and I beheld,
With an astonishment but ill suppressed,
His ghostly figure moving at my side;
Nor could I, while we journeyed thus, forbear 435
To turn from present hardships to the past,
And speak of war, battle, and pestilence,
Sprinkling this talk with questions, better spared,
On what he might himself have seen or felt.
He all the while was in demeanour calm, 440
Concise in answer; solemn and sublime
He might have seemed, but that in all he said
There was a strange half-absence, as of one
Knowing too well the importance of his theme,
But feeling it no longer. Our discourse 445
Soon ended, and together on we passed
In silence through a wood gloomy and still.
Up-turning, then, along an open field,
We reached a cottage. At the door I knocked,
And earnestly to charitable care 450
Commended him as a poor friendless man,
Belated and by sickness overcome.
Assured that now the traveller would repose
In comfort, I entreated that henceforth
He would not linger in the public ways, 455
But ask for timely furtherance and help
Such as his state required. At this reproof,
With the same ghastly mildness in his look,
He said, 'My trust is in the God of Heaven,
And in the eye of him who passes me!' 460
    The cottage door was speedily unbarred,
And now the soldier touched his hat once more

With his lean hand, and in a faltering voice,
Whose tone bespake reviving interests
Till then unfelt, he thanked me; I returned　　465
The farewell blessing of the patient man,
And so we parted. Back I cast a look,
And lingered near the door a little space,
Then sought with quiet heart my distant home.

Book VI. Cambridge and the Alps

Written 1804

YET still in me with those soft luxuries
Mixed something of stern mood, an under-thirst
Of vigour seldom utterly allayed.
And from that source how different a sadness　　560
Would issue, let one incident make known.
When from the Vallais we had turned, and clomb
Along the Simplon's steep and rugged road,
Following a band of muleteers, we reached
A halting-place, where all together took　　565
Their noon-tide meal. Hastily rose our guide,
Leaving us at the board; awhile we lingered,
Then paced the beaten downward way that led
Right to a rough stream's edge, and there broke off;
The only track now visible was one　　570
That from the torrent's further brink held forth
Conspicuous invitation to ascend
A lofty mountain. After brief delay
Crossing the unbridged stream, that road we took,
And clomb with eagerness, till anxious fears　　575
Intruded, for we failed to overtake

Our comrades gone before. By fortunate chance,
While every moment added doubt to doubt,
A peasant met us, from whose mouth we learned
That to the spot which had perplexed us first 580
We must descend, and there should find the road,
Which in the stony channel of the stream
Lay a few steps, and then along its banks;
And, that our future course, all plain to sight,
Was downwards, with the current of that stream. 585
Loth to believe what we so grieved to hear,
For still we had hopes that pointed to the clouds,
We questioned him again, and yet again;
But every word that from the peasant's lips
Came in reply, translated by our feelings, 590
Ended in this,—*that we had crossed the Alps.*

  Imagination—here the Power so called
Through sad incompetence of human speech,
That awful Power rose from the mind's abyss
Like an unfathered vapour that enwraps, 595
At once, some lonely traveller. I was lost;
Halted without an effort to break through;
But to my conscious soul I now can say—
'I recognise thy glory:' in such strength
Of usurpation, when the light of sense 600
Goes out, but with a flash that has revealed
The invisible world, doth greatness make abode,
There harbours; whether we be young or old,
Our destiny, our being's heart and home,
Is with infinitude, and only there; 605
With hope it is, hope that can never die,
Effort, and expectation, and desire,
And something evermore about to be.
Under such banners militant, the soul

Seeks for no trophies, struggles for no spoils   610
That may attest her prowess, blest in thoughts
That are their own perfection and reward,
Strong in herself and in beatitude
That hides her, like the mighty flood of Nile
Poured from his fount of Abyssinian clouds   615
To fertilise the whole Egyptian plain.

   The melancholy slackening that ensued
Upon those tidings by the peasant given
Was soon dislodged. Downwards we hurried fast,
And, with the half-shaped road which we had missed, 620
Entered a narrow chasm. The brook and road
Were fellow-travellers in this gloomy strait,
And with them did we journey several hours
At a slow pace. The immeasurable height
Of woods decaying, never to be decayed,   625
The stationary blasts of waterfalls,
And in the narrow rent at every turn
Winds thwarting winds, bewildered and forlorn,
The torrents shooting from the clear blue sky,
The rocks that muttered close upon our ears,   630
Black drizzling crags that spake by the way-side
As if a voice were in them, the sick sight
And giddy prospect of the raving stream,
The unfettered clouds and region of the Heavens,
Tumult and peace, the darkness and the light—   635
Were all like workings of one mind, the features
Of the same face, blossoms upon one tree;
Characters of the great Apocalypse,
The types and symbols of Eternity,
Of first, and last, and midst, and without end. . . .   640

Book VIII. Retrospect

Written 1804

YET, hail to you
Moors, mountains, headlands, and ye hollow vales,
Ye long deep channels for the Atlantic's voice,
Powers of my native region! Ye that seize
The heart with firmer grasp! Your snows and streams
Ungovernable, and your terrifying winds,   220
That howl so dismally for him who treads
Companionless your awful solitudes!
There, 'tis the shepherd's task the winter long
To wait upon the storms: of their approach
Sagacious, into sheltering coves he drives   225
His flock, and thither from the homestead bears
A toilsome burden up the craggy ways,
And deals it out, their regular nourishment
Strewn on the frozen snow. And when the spring
Looks out, and all the pastures dance with lambs,   230
And when the flock, with warmer weather, climbs
Higher and higher, him his office leads
To watch their goings, whatsoever track
The wanderers choose. For this he quits his home
At day-spring, and no sooner doth the sun   235
Begin to strike him with a fire-like heat,
Than he lies down upon some shining rock,
And breakfasts with his dog. When they have stolen,
As is their wont, a pittance from strict time,
For rest not needed or exchange of love,   240
Then from his couch he starts; and now his feet
Crush out a livelier fragrance from the flowers
Of lowly thyme, by Nature's skill enwrought

In the wild turf: the lingering dews of morn
Smoke round him, as from hill to hill he hies,   245
His staff protending like a hunter's spear,
Or by its aid leaping from crag to crag,
And o'er the brawling beds of unbridged streams.
Philosophy, methinks, at Fancy's call,
Might deign to follow him through what he does   250
Or sees in his day's march; himself he feels,
In those vast regions where his service lies,
A freeman, wedded to his life of hope
And hazard, and hard labour interchanged
With that majestic indolence so dear   255
To native man. A rambling school-boy, thus
I felt his presence in his own domain,
As of a lord and master, or a power,
Or genius, under Nature, under God,
Presiding; and severest solitude   260
Had more commanding looks when he was there.
When up the lonely brooks on rainy days
Angling I went, or trod the trackless hills
By mists bewildered, suddenly mine eyes
Have glanced upon him distant a few steps,   265
In size a giant, stalking through thick fog,
His sheep like Greenland bears; or, as he stepped
Beyond the boundary line of some hill-shadow,
His form hath flashed upon me, glorified
By the deep radiance of the setting sun: 270
Or him have I descried in distant sky,
A solitary object and sublime,
Above all height! like an aerial cross
Stationed alone upon a spiry rock
Of the Chartreuse, for worship. Thus was man   275
Ennobled outwardly before my sight,

And thus my heart was early introduced
To an unconscious love and reverence
Of human nature; hence the human form
To me became an index of delight,   280
Of grace and honour, power and worthiness.
Meanwhile this creature—spiritual almost
As those of books, but more exalted far;
Far more of an imaginative form
Than the gay Corin of the groves, who lives   285
For his own fancies, or to dance by the hour,
In coronal, with Phyllis in the midst—
Was, for the purposes of kind, a man
With the most common; husband, father; learned,
Could teach, admonish; suffered with the rest   290
From vice and folly, wretchedness and fear;
Of this I little saw, cared less for it,
But something must have felt. . . .

But when that first poetic faculty   365
Of plain Imagination and severe,
No longer a mute influence of the soul,
Ventured, at some rash Muse's earnest call,
To try her strength among harmonious words;
And to book-notions and the rules of art   370
Did knowingly conform itself; there came
Among the simple shapes of human life
A wilfulness of fancy and conceit;
And Nature and her objects beautified
These fictions, as in some sort, in their turn,   375
They burnished her. From touch of this new power
Nothing was safe: the elder-tree that grew
Beside the well-known charnel-house had then
A dismal look: the yew-tree had its ghost,

That took his station there for ornament: 380
The dignities of plain occurrence then
Were tasteless, and truth's golden mean, a point
Where no sufficient pleasure could be found.
Then, if a widow, staggering with the blow
Of her distress, was known to have turned her steps 385
To the cold grave in which her husband slept,
One night, or haply more than one, through pain
Or half-insensate impotence of mind,
The fact was caught at greedily, and there
She must be visitant the whole year through,   390
Wetting the turf with never-ending tears.
    Through quaint obliquities I might pursue
These cravings; when the fox-glove, one by one,
Upwards through every stage of the tall stem,
Had shed beside the public way its bells,   395
And stood of all dismantled, save the last
Left at the tapering ladder's top, that seemed
To bend as doth a slender blade of grass
Tipped with a rain-drop, Fancy loved to seat,
Beneath the plant despoiled, but crested still   400
With this last relic, soon itself to fall,
Some vagrant mother, whose arch little ones,
All unconcerned by her dejected plight,
Laughed as with rival eagerness their hands
Gathered the purple cups that round them lay,   405
Strewing the turf's green slope. . . .
Thus wilful Fancy, in no hurtful mood,   421
Engrafted far-fetched shapes on feelings bred
By pure Imagination: busy Power
She was, and with her ready pupil turned
Instinctively to human passions, then   425
Least understood. Yet, 'mid the fervent swarm

Of these vagaries, with an eye so rich
As mine was through the bounty of a grand
And lovely region, I had forms distinct
To steady me: each airy thought revolved   430
Round a substantial centre, which at once
Incited it to motion, and controlled. . . .

Book XI. France

Written 1800?

A VEIL had been
Uplifted; why deceive ourselves? in sooth,
'Twas even so; and sorrow for the man
Who either had not eyes wherewith to see,
Or, seeing, had forgotten! A strong shock   270
Was given to old opinions; all men's minds
Had felt its power, and mine was both let loose,
Let loose and goaded. After what hath been
Already said of patriotic love,
Suffice it here to add, that, somewhat stern   275
In temperament, withal a happy man,
And therefore bold to look on painful things,
Free likewise of the world, and thence more bold,
I summoned my best skill, and toiled, intent
To anatomise the frame of social life,   280
Yea, the whole body of society
Searched to its heart. Share with me, Friend! the wish
That some dramatic tale, endued with shapes
Livelier, and flinging out less guarded words
Than suit the work we fashion, might set forth   285
What then I learned, or think I learned, of truth,
And the errors into which I fell, betrayed

By present objects, and by reasonings false
From their beginnings, inasmuch as drawn
Out of a heart that had been turned aside   290
From Nature's way by outward accidents,
And which was thus confounded, more and more
Misguided, and misguiding. So I fared,
Dragging all precepts, judgments, maxims, creeds,
Like culprits to the bar; calling the mind,   295
Suspiciously, to establish in plain day
Her titles and her honours; now believing,
Now disbelieving; endlessly perplexed
With impulse, motive, right and wrong, the ground
Of obligation, what the rule and whence   300
The sanction; till, demanding formal *proof*,
And seeking it in every thing, I lost
All feeling of conviction, and, in fine,
Sick, wearied out with contrarieties,
Yielded up moral questions in despair. . . .   305

Book XII. Imagination and Taste

Written 1805

THERE are in our existence spots of time,
That with distinct pre-eminence retain
A renovating virtue, whence, depressed   210
By false opinion and contentious thought,
Or aught of heavier or more deadly weight,
In trivial occupations, and the round
Of ordinary intercourse, our minds
Are nourished and invisibly repaired;   215
A virtue, by which pleasure is enhanced,

That penetrates, enables us to mount,
When high, more high, and lifts us up when fallen.
This efficacious spirit chiefly lurks
Among those passages of life that give   220
Profoundest knowledge to what point, and how,
The mind is lord and master—outward sense
The obedient servant of her will. Such moments
Are scattered everywhere, taking their date
From our first childhood. I remember well,   225
That once, while yet my inexperienced hand
Could scarcely hold a bridle, with proud hopes
I mounted, and we journeyed towards the hills:
An ancient servant of my father's house
Was with me, my encourager and guide: 230
We had not travelled long, ere some mischance
Disjoined me from my comrade; and, through fear
Dismounting, down the rough and stony moor
I led my horse, and, stumbling on, at length
Came to a bottom, where in former times   235
A murderer had been hung in iron chains.
The gibbet-mast had mouldered down, the bones
And iron case were gone; but on the turf,
Hard by, soon after that fell deed was wrought,
Some unknown hand had carved the murderer's name.   240
The monumental letters were inscribed
In times long past; but still, from year to year,
By superstition of the neighbourhood,
The grass is cleared away, and to this hour
The characters are fresh and visible: 245
A casual glance had shown them, and I fled,
Faltering and faint, and ignorant of the road:
Then, reascending the bare common, saw
A naked pool that lay beneath the hills,

The beacon on the summit, and, more near,   250
A girl, who bore a pitcher on her head,
And seemed with difficult steps to force her way
Against the blowing wind. It was, in truth,
An ordinary sight; but I should need
Colours and words that are unknown to man,   255
To paint the visionary dreariness
Which, while I looked all round for my lost guide,
Invested moorland waste, and naked pool,
The beacon crowning the lone eminence,
The female and her garments vexed and tossed   260
By the strong wind. When, in the blessed hours
Of early love, the loved one at my side,
I roamed, in daily presence of this scene,
Upon the naked pool and dreary crags,
And on the melancholy beacon fell   265
A spirit of pleasure and youth's golden gleam;
And think ye not with radiance more sublime
For these remembrances, and for the power
They had left behind? So feeling comes in aid
Of feeling, and diversity of strength   270
Attends us, if but once we have been strong.
Oh! mystery of man, from what a depth
Proceed thy honours. I am lost, but see
In simple childhood something of the base
On which thy greatness stands; but this I feel,   275
That from thyself it comes, that thou must give,
Else never canst receive. The days gone by
Return upon me almost from the dawn
Of life; the hiding-places of man's power
Open; I would approach them, but they close.   280
I see my glimpses now; when age comes on,
May scarcely see at all; and I would give,

While yet we may, as far as words can give,
Substance and life to what I feel, enshrining,
Such is my hope, the spirit of the Past   285
For future restoration. . . .

Book XIV. Conclusion

Written 1804

In one of those excursions (may they ne'er
Fade from remembrance!) through the Northern tracts
Of Cambria ranging with a youthful friend,
I left Bethgelert's huts at couching-time,
And westward took my way, to see the sun   5
Rise from the top of Snowdon. To the door
Of a rude cottage at the mountain's base
We came, and roused the shepherd who attends
The adventurous stranger's steps, a trusty guide;
Then, cheered by short refreshment, sallied forth.   10

It was a close, warm, breezeless summer night,
Wan, dull, and glaring, with a dripping fog
Low-hung and thick that covered all the sky;
But, undiscouraged, we began to climb
The mountain-side. The mist soon girt us round,   15
And, after ordinary travellers' talk
With our conductor, pensively we sank
Each into commerce with his private thoughts:
Thus did we breast the ascent, and by myself
Was nothing either seen or heard that checked   20
Those musings or diverted, save that once
The shepherd's lurcher, who, among the crags,
Had to his joy unearthed a hedgehog, teased
His coiled-up prey with barkings turbulent.

This small adventure, for even such it seemed   25
In that wild place and at the dead of night,
Being over and forgotten, on we wound
In silence as before. With forehead bent
Earthward, as if in opposition set
Against an enemy, I panted up   30
With eager pace, and no less eager thoughts.
Thus might we wear a midnight hour away,
Ascending at loose distance each from each,
And I, as chanced, the foremost of the band:
When at my feet the ground appeared to brighten,   35
And with a step or two seemed brighter still;
Nor was time given to ask or learn the cause,
For instantly a light upon the turf
Fell like a flash, and lo! as I looked up,
The Moon hung naked in a firmament   40
Of azure without cloud, and at my feet
Rested a silent sea of hoary mist.
A hundred hills their dusky backs upheaved
All over this still ocean; and beyond,
Far, far beyond, the solid vapours stretched,   45
In headlands, tongues, and promontory shapes,
Into the main Atlantic, that appeared
To dwindle, and give up his majesty,
Usurped upon far as the sight could reach.
Not so the ethereal vault; encroachment none   50
Was there, nor loss; only the inferior stars
Had disappeared, or shed a fainter light
In the clear presence of the full-orbed Moon,
Who, from her sovereign elevation, gazed
Upon the billowy ocean, as it lay   55
All meek and silent, save that through a rift—
Not distant from the shore whereon we stood,

A fixed, abysmal, gloomy, breathing-place—
Mounted the roar of waters, torrents, streams
Innumerable, roaring with one voice!   60
Heard over earth and sea, and, in that hour,
For so it seemed, felt by the starry heavens.
  When into air had partially dissolved
That vision, given to spirits of the night
And three chance human wanderers, in calm thought 65
Reflected, it appeared to me the type
Of a majestic intellect, its acts
And its possessions, what it has and craves,
What in itself it is, and would become.
There I beheld the emblem of a mind   70
That feeds upon infinity, that broods
Over the dark abyss, intent to hear
Its voices issuing forth to silent light
In one continuous stream; a mind sustained
By recognitions of transcendent power,   75
In sense conducting to ideal form,
In soul of more than mortal privilege.
One function, above all, of such a mind
Had Nature shadowed there, by putting forth,
'Mid circumstances awful and sublime,   80
That mutual domination which she loves
To exert upon the face of outward things,
So moulded, joined, abstracted, so endowed
With interchangeable supremacy,
That men, least sensitive, see, hear, perceive,   85
And cannot choose but feel. The power, which all
Acknowledge when thus moved, which Nature thus
To bodily sense exhibits, is the express
Resemblance of that glorious faculty
That higher minds bear with them as their own. . . .   90

The Old Cumberland Beggar

Written 1797. *Lyrical Ballads* (1800)

The class of Beggars, to which the Old Man here described belongs, will probably soon be extinct. It consisted of poor, and, mostly, old and infirm persons, who confined themselves to a stated round in their neighbourhood, and had certain fixed days, on which, at different houses, they regularly received alms, sometimes in money, but mostly in provisions.

I SAW an aged Beggar in my walk;
And he was seated, by the highway side,
On a low structure of rude masonry
Built at the foot of a huge hill, that they
Who lead their horses down the steep rough road   5
May thence remount at ease. The aged Man
Had placed his staff across the broad smooth stone
That overlays the pile; and, from a bag
All white with flour, the dole of village dames,
He drew his scraps and fragments, one by one;   10
And scanned them with a fixed and serious look
Of idle computation. In the sun,
Upon the second step of that small pile,
Surrounded by those wild unpeopled hills,
He sat, and ate his food in solitude: 15
And ever, scattered from his palsied hand,
That, still attempting to prevent the waste,
Was baffled still, the crumbs in little showers
Fell on the ground; and the small mountain birds,
Not venturing yet to peck their destined meal,   20
Approached within the length of half his staff.
  Him from my childhood have I known; and then
He was so old, he seems not older now;

He travels on, a solitary Man,
So helpless in appearance, that for him   25
The sauntering Horseman throws not with a slack
And careless hand his alms upon the ground,
But stops,—that he may safely lodge the coin
Within the old Man's hat; nor quits him so,
But still, when he has given his horse the rein,   30
Watches the aged Beggar with a look
Sidelong, and half-reverted. She who tends
The toll-gate, when in summer at her door
She turns her wheel, if on the road she sees
The aged Beggar coming, quits her work,   35
And lifts the latch for him that he may pass.
The post-boy, when his rattling wheels o'ertake
The aged Beggar in the woody lane,
Shouts to him from behind; and, if thus warned
The old man does not change his course, the boy   40
Turns with less noisy wheels to the roadside,
And passes gently by, without a curse
Upon his lips or anger at his heart.
    He travels on, a solitary Man;
His age has no companion. On the ground   45
His eyes are turned, and, as he moves along,
They move along the ground; and, evermore,
Instead of common and habitual sight
Of fields with rural works, of hill and dale,
And the blue sky, one little span of earth   50
Is all his prospect. Thus, from day to day.
Bow-bent, his eyes for ever on the ground,
He plies his weary journey; seeing still,
And seldom knowing that he sees, some straw,
Some scattered leaf, or marks which, in one track,   55
The nails of cart or chariot-wheel have left

Impressed on the white road,—in the same line,
At distance still the same. Poor Traveller!
His staff trails with him; scarcely do his feet
Disturb the summer dust; he is so still   60
In look and motion, that the cottage curs,
Ere he has passed the door, will turn away,
Weary of barking at him. Boys and girls,
The vacant and the busy, maids and youths,
The urchins newly breeched—all pass him by: 65
Him even the slow-paced waggon leaves behind.
    But deem not this Man useless—Statesmen! ye
Who are so restless in your wisdom, ye
Who have a broom still ready in your hands
To rid the world of nuisances; ye proud,   70
Heart-swoln, while in your pride ye contemplate
Your talents, power, or wisdom, deem him not
A burthen of the earth! 'Tis Nature's law
That none, the meanest of created things,
Of forms created the most vile and brute,   75
The dullest or most noxious, should exist
Divorced from good—a spirit and pulse of good,
A life and soul, to every mode of being
Inseparably linked. Then be assured
That least of all can aught—that ever owned   80
The heaven-regarding eye and front sublime
Which man is born to—sink, howe'er depressed,
So low as to be scorned without a sin;
Without offence to God cast out of view;
Like the dry remnant of a garden-flower   85
Whose seeds are shed, or as an implement
Worn out and worthless. While from door to door,
This old Man creeps, the villagers in him
Behold a record which together binds

Past deeds and offices of charity,   90
Else unremembered, and so keeps alive
The kindly mood in hearts which lapse of years,
And that half-wisdom half-experience gives,
Make slow to feel, and by sure steps resign
To selfishness and cold oblivious cares.   95
Among the farms and solitary huts,
Hamlets and thinly-scattered villages,
Where'er the aged Beggar takes his rounds,
The mild necessity of use compels
To acts of love; and habit does the work   100
Of reason; yet prepares that after-joy
Which reason cherishes. And thus the soul,
By that sweet taste of pleasure unpursued,
Doth find herself insensibly disposed
To virtue and true goodness. Some there are,   105
By their good works exalted, lofty minds,
And meditative, authors of delight
And happiness, which to the end of time
Will live, and spread, and kindle; even such minds
In childhood, from this solitary Being,   110
Or from like wanderer, haply have received
(A thing more precious far than all that books
Of the solicitudes of love can do!)
That first mild touch of sympathy and thought,
In which they found their kindred with a world   115
Where want and sorrow were. The easy man
Who sits at his own door,—and, like the pear
That overhangs his head from the green wall,
Feeds in the sunshine; the robust and young,
The prosperous and unthinking, they who live   120
Sheltered, and flourish in a little grove
Of their own kindred;—all behold in him

A silent monitor, which on their minds
Must needs impress a transitory thought
Of self-congratulation, to the heart   125
Of each recalling his peculiar boons,
His charters and exemptions; and, perchance,
Though he to no one give the fortitude
And circumspection needful to preserve
His present blessings, and to husband up   130
The respite of the season, he, at least,
And 'tis no vulgar service, makes them felt.
     Yet further.———Many, I believe, there are
Who live a life of virtuous decency,
Men who can hear the Decalogue and feel   135
No self-reproach; who of the moral law
Established in the land where they abide
Are strict observers; and not negligent
In acts of love to those with whom they dwell,
Their kindred, and the children of their blood.   140
Praise be to such, and to their slumbers peace!
—But of the poor man ask, the abject poor;
Go, and demand of him, if there be here
In this cold abstinence from evil deeds,
And these inevitable charities,   145
Wherewith to satisfy the human soul?
No—man is dear to man; the poorest poor
Long for some moments in a weary life
When they can know and feel that they have been,
Themselves, the fathers and the dealers-out   150
Of some small blessings; have been kind to such
As needed kindness, for this single cause,
That we have all of us one human heart.
—Such pleasure is to one kind Being known,
My neighbour, when with punctual care, each week, 155

Duly as Friday comes, though pressed herself
By her own wants, she from her store of meal
Takes one unsparing handful for the scrip
Of this old Mendicant, and, from her door
Returning with exhilarated heart,   160
Sits by her fire, and builds her hope in heaven.
  Then let him pass, a blessing on his head!
And while in that vast solitude to which
The tide of things has borne him, he appears
To breathe and live but for himself alone,   165
Unblamed, uninjured, let him bear about
The good which the benignant law of Heaven
Has hung around him: and, while life is his,
Still let him prompt the unlettered villagers
To tender offices and pensive thoughts.   170
—Then let him pass, a blessing on his head!
And, long as he can wander, let him breathe
The freshness of the valleys; let his blood
Struggle with frosty air and winter snows;
And let the chartered wind that sweeps the heath   175
Beat his grey locks against his withered face.
Reverence the hope whose vital anxiousness
Gives the last human interest to his heart.
May never HOUSE, misnamed of INDUSTRY,
Make him a captive!—for that pent-up din,   180
Those life-consuming sounds that clog the air,
Be his the natural silence of old age!
Let him be free of mountain solitudes;
And have around him, whether heard or not,
The pleasant melody of woodland birds.   185
Few are his pleasures; if his eyes have now
Been doomed so long to settle upon earth
That not without some effort they behold

The countenance of the horizontal sun,
Rising or setting, let the light at least   190
Find a free entrance to their languid orbs,
And let him, *where* and *when* he will, sit down
Beneath the trees, or on a grassy bank
Of highway side, and with the little birds
Share his chance-gathered meal; and, finally,   195
As in the eye of Nature he has lived,
So in the eye of Nature let him die!

Animal Tranquillity and Decay

Written 1797

THE little hedgerow birds,
That peck along the road, regard him not.
He travels on, and in his face, his step,
His gait, is one expression: every limb,
His look and bending figure, all bespeak   5
A man who does not move with pain, but moves
With thought.—He is insensibly subdued
To settled quiet: he is one by whom
All effort seems forgotten; one to whom
Long patience hath such mild composure given,   10
That patience now doth seem a thing of which
He hath no need. He is by nature led
To peace so perfect that the young behold
With envy, what the Old Man hardly feels.

Goody Blake and Harry Gill

A TRUE STORY

Written 1798

Oʜ! what's the matter? what's the matter?
What is't that ails young Harry Gill?
That evermore his teeth they chatter,
Chatter, chatter, chatter still!
Of waistcoats Harry has no lack,   5
Good duffle grey, and flannel fine;
He has a blanket on his back,
And coats enough to smother nine.

In March, December, and in July,
'Tis all the same with Harry Gill;   10
The neighbours tell, and tell you truly,
His teeth they chatter, chatter still.
At night, at morning, and at noon,
'Tis all the same with Harry Gill;
Beneath the sun, beneath the moon,   15
His teeth they chatter, chatter still!

Young Harry was a lusty drover,
And who so stout of limb as he?
His cheeks were red as ruddy clover;
His voice was like the voice of three.   20
Old Goody Blake was old and poor;
Ill fed she was, and thinly clad;
And any man who passed her door
Might see how poor a hut she had.

All day she spun in her poor dwelling: 25
And then her three hours' work at night,
Alas! 'twas hardly worth the telling,
It would not pay for candle-light.
Remote from sheltered village-green,
On a hill's northern side she dwelt,   30
Where from sea-blasts the hawthorns lean,
And hoary dews are slow to melt.

By the same fire to boil their pottage,
Two poor old Dames, as I have known,
Will often live in one small cottage;   35
But she, poor Woman! housed alone.
'Twas well enough, when summer came,
The long, warm, lightsome summer-day,
Then at her door the *canty* Dame
Would sit, as any linnet, gay.   40

But when the ice our streams did fetter,
Oh then how her old bones would shake!
You would have said, if you had met her,
'Twas a hard time for Goody Blake,
Her evenings then were dull and dead: 45
Sad case it was, as you may think,
For very cold to go to bed;
And then for cold not sleep a wink.

O joy for her! whene'er in winter
The winds at night had made a rout;   50
And scattered many a lusty splinter
And many a rotten bough about.
Yet never had she, well or sick,
As every man who knew her says,
A pile beforehand, turf or stick,   55
Enough to warm her for three days.

Now, when the frost was past enduring,
And made her poor old bones to ache,
Could any thing be more alluring
Than an old hedge to Goody Blake?   60
And, now and then, it must be said,
When her old bones were cold and chill,
She left her fire, or left her bed,
To seek the hedge of Harry Gill.

Now Harry he had long suspected   65
This trespass of old Goody Blake;
And vowed that she should be detected—
That he on her would vengeance take.
And oft from his warm fire he'd go,
And to the fields his road would take;   70
And there, at night, in frost and snow,
He watched to seize old Goody Blake.

And once, behind a rick of barley,
Thus looking out did Harry stand:
The moon was full and shining clearly,   75
And crisp with frost the stubble land.
—He hears a noise—he's all awake—
Again?—on tip-toe down the hill
He softly creeps—'tis Goody Blake;
She's at the hedge of Harry Gill!   80

Right glad was he when he beheld her:
Stick after stick did Goody pull:
He stood behind a bush of elder,
Till she had filled her apron full.
When with her load she turned about,   85
The by-way back again to take;
He started forward, with a shout,
And sprang upon poor Goody Blake.

And fiercely by the arm he took her,
And by the arm he held her fast,   90
And fiercely by the arm he shook her,
And cried, 'I've caught you then at last!'
Then Goody, who had nothing said,
Her bundle from her lap let fall;
And, kneeling on the sticks, she prayed   95
To God that is the judge of all.

She prayed, her withered hand uprearing,
While Harry held her by the arm—
'God! who art never out of hearing,
O may he never more be warm!'   100
The cold, cold moon above her head,
Thus on her knees did Goody pray;
Young Harry heard what she had said:
And icy cold he turned away.

He went complaining all the morrow   105
That he was cold and very chill:
His face was gloom, his heart was sorrow,
Alas! that day for Harry Gill!
That day he wore a riding-coat,
But not a whit the warmer he: 110
Another was on Thursday brought,
And ere the Sabbath he had three.

'Twas all in vain, a useless matter,
And blankets were about him pinned;
Yet still his jaws and teeth they clatter,   115
Like a loose casement in the wind.
And Harry's flesh it fell away;
And all who see him say, 'tis plain,
That, live as long as live he may,
He never will be warm again.   120

No word to any man he utters,
A-bed or up, to young or old;
But ever to himself he mutters,
'Poor Harry Gill is very cold.'
A-bed or up, by night or day;   125
His teeth they chatter, chatter still.
Now think, ye farmers all, I pray,
Of Goody Blake and Harry Gill!

Simon Lee

THE OLD HUNTSMAN

With an incident in which he was concerned

Written 1798

In the sweet shire of Cardigan,
Not far from pleasant Ivor-hall,
An old Man dwells, a little man,—
'Tis said he once was tall.
Full five-and-thirty years he lived   5
A running huntsman merry;
And still the centre of his cheek
Is red as a ripe cherry.

No man like him the horn could sound,
And hill and valley rang with glee   10
When Echo bandied, round and round,
The halloo of Simon Lee.
In those proud days, he little cared
For husbandry or tillage;
To blither tasks did Simon rouse   15
The sleepers of the village.

He all the country could outrun,
Could leave both man and horse behind;
And often, ere the chase was done,
He reeled, and was stone-blind.   20
And still there's something in the world
At which his heart rejoices;
For when the chiming hounds are out,
He dearly loves their voices!

But, oh the heavy change!—bereft   25
Of health, strength, friends, and kindred, see!
Old Simon to the world is left
In liveried poverty.
His Master's dead,—and no one now
Dwells in the Hall of Ivor;   30
Men, dogs, and horses, all are dead;
He is the sole survivor.

And he is lean and he is sick;
His body, dwindled and awry,
Rests upon ankles swoln and thick;   35
His legs are thin and dry.
One prop he has, and only one,
His wife, an aged woman,
Lives with him, near the waterfall,
Upon the village Common.   40

Beside their moss-grown hut of clay,
Not twenty paces from the door,
A scrap of land they have, but they
Are poorest of the poor.
This scrap of land he from the heath   45
Enclosed when he was stronger;
But what to them avails the land
Which he can till no longer?

Oft, working by her Husband's side,
Ruth does what Simon cannot do;   50
For she, with scanty cause for pride,
Is stouter of the two.
And, though you with your utmost skill
From labour could not wean them,
'Tis little, very little—all   55
That they can do between them.

Few months of life has he in store
As he to you will tell,
For still, the more he works, the more
Do his weak ankles swell.   60
My gentle Reader, I perceive
How patiently you've waited,
And now I fear that you expect
Some tale will be related.

O Reader! had you in your mind   65
Such stores as silent thought can bring,
O gentle Reader! you would find
A tale in every thing.
What more I have to say is short,
And you must kindly take it: 70
It is no tale; but, should you think,
Perhaps a tale you'll make it.

One summer-day I chanced to see
This old Man doing all he could
To unearth the root of an old tree,   75
A stump of rotten wood.
The mattock tottered in his hand;
So vain was his endeavour,
That at the root of the old tree
He might have worked for ever.   80

'You're overtasked, good Simon Lee,
Give me your tool,' to him I said;
And at the word right gladly he
Received my proffered aid.
I struck, and with a single blow   85
The tangled root I severed,
At which the poor old Man so long
And vainly had endeavoured.

The tears into his eyes were brought,
And thanks and praises seemed to run   90
So fast out of his heart, I thought
They never would have done.
—I've heard of hearts unkind, kind deeds
With coldness still returning;
Alas! the gratitude of men   95
Hath oftener left me mourning.

Anecdote for Fathers

'Retine vim istam, falsa enim dicam, si coges.' EUSEBIUS.

Written 1798

I HAVE a boy of five years old;
His face is fair and fresh to see;
His limbs are cast in beauty's mould,
And dearly he loves me.

One morn we strolled on our dry walk,   5
Our quiet home all full in view,
And held such intermitted talk
As we are wont to do.

My thoughts on former pleasures ran;
I thought of Kilve's delightful shore,   10
Our pleasant home when spring began,
A long, long year before.

A day it was when I could bear
Some fond regrets to entertain;
With so much happiness to spare,   15
I could not feel a pain.

The green earth echoed to the feet
Of lambs that bounded through the glade,
From shade to sunshine, and as fleet
From sunshine back to shade.   20

Birds warbled round me—and each trace
Of inward sadness had its charm;
Kilve, thought I, was a favoured place,
And so is Liswyn farm.

My boy beside me tripped, so slim   25
And graceful in his rustic dress!
And, as we talked, I questioned him,
In very idleness.

'Now tell me, had you rather be,'
I said, and took him by the arm,   30
'On Kilve's smooth shore, by the green sea,
Or here at Liswyn farm?'

In careless mood he looked at me,
While still I held him by the arm,
And said, 'At Kilve I'd rather be   35
Than here at Liswyn farm.'

'Now, little Edward, say why so:
My little Edward, tell me why.'—
'I cannot tell, I do not know.'—
'Why, this is strange,' said I;   40

'For here are woods, hills smooth and warm:
There surely must some reason be
Why you would change sweet Liswyn farm
For Kilve by the green sea.'

At this my boy hung down his head,   45
He blushed with shame, nor made reply;
And three times to the child I said,
'Why, Edward, tell me why?'

His head he raised—there was in sight,
It caught his eye, he saw it plain—   50
Upon the house-top, glittering bright,
A broad and gilded vane.

Then did the boy his tongue unlock,
And eased his mind with this reply:
'At Kilve there was no weather-cock;   55
And that's the reason why.'

O dearest, dearest boy! my heart
For better lore would seldom yearn,
Could I but teach the hundredth part
Of what from thee I learn.   60

We are Seven

Written 1798

——A SIMPLE Child,
That lightly draws its breath,
And feels its life in every limb,
What should it know of death?

I met a little cottage Girl;   5
She was eight years old, she said;
Her hair was thick with many a curl
That clustered round her head.

She had a rustic, woodland air,
And she was wildly clad: 10
Her eyes were fair, and very fair;
—Her beauty made me glad.

'Sisters and brothers, little maid,
How many may you be?'
'How many? Seven in all,' she said,   15
And wondering looked at me.

'And where are they? I pray you tell.'
She answered, 'Seven are we;
And two of us at Conway dwell,
And two are gone to sea.   20

'Two of us in the church-yard lie,
My sister and my brother;
And, in the church-yard cottage, I
Dwell near them with my mother.'

'You say that two at Conway dwell,   25
And two are gone to sea,
Yet ye are seven! I pray you tell,
Sweet Maid, how this may be.'

Then did the little Maid reply,
'Seven boys and girls are we;   30
Two of us in the church-yard lie,
Beneath the church-yard tree.'

'You run about, my little Maid,
Your limbs they are alive;
If two are in the church-yard laid,   35
Then ye are only five.'

'Their graves are green, they may be seen.'
The little Maid replied,
'Twelve steps or more from my mother's door,
And they are side by side.   40

'My stockings there I often knit,
My kerchief there I hem;
And there upon the ground I sit,
And sing a song to them.

'And often after sun-set, Sir,   45
When it is light and fair,
I take my little porringer,
And eat my supper there.

'The first that died was sister Jane;
In bed she moaning lay,   50
Till God released her of her pain;
And then she went away.

'So in the church-yard she was laid;
And, when the grass was dry,
Together round her grave we played,   55
My brother John and I.

'And when the ground was white with snow,
And I could run and slide,
My brother John was forced to go,
And he lies by her side.'   60

'How many are you, then,' said I,
'If they two are in heaven?'
Quick was the little Maid's reply,
'O Master! we are seven.'

'But they are dead; those two are dead!   65
Their spirits are in heaven!'
'Twas throwing words away; for still
The little Maid would have her will,
And said, 'Nay, we are seven!'

Expostulation and Reply

Written 1798

'Why, William, on that old grey stone,
Thus for the length of half a day,
Why, William, sit you thus alone,
And dream your time away?

'Where are your books?—that light bequeathed   5
To Beings else forlorn and blind!
Up! up! and drink the spirit breathed
From dead men to their kind.

'You look round on your Mother Earth,
As if she for no purpose bore you;   10
As if you were her first-born birth,
And none had lived before you!'

One morning thus, by Esthwaite lake,
When life was sweet, I knew not why,
To me my good friend Matthew spake,   15
And thus I made reply:

'The eye—it cannot choose but see;
We cannot bid the ear be still;
Our bodies feel, where'er they be,
Against or with our will.   20

'Nor less I deem that there are Powers
Which of themselves our minds impress;
That we can feed this mind of ours
In a wise passiveness.

'Think you, 'mid all this mighty sum   25
Of things for ever speaking,
That nothing of itself will come,
But we must still be seeking?

'—Then ask not wherefore, here, alone,
Conversing as I may,   30
I sit upon this old grey stone,
And dream my time away.'

The Tables Turned

AN EVENING SCENE ON THE SAME SUBJECT

Written 1798

Up! up! my Friend, and quit your books;
Or surely you'll grow double:
Up! up! my Friend, and clear your looks;
Why all this toil and trouble?

The sun, above the mountain's head,   5
A freshening lustre mellow
Through all the long green fields has spread,
His first sweet evening yellow.

Books! 'tis a dull and endless strife:
Come, hear the woodland linnet,   10
How sweet his music! on my life,
There's more of wisdom in it.

And hark! how blithe the throstle sings!
He, too, is no mean preacher:
Come forth into the light of things,   15
Let Nature be your Teacher.

She has a world of ready wealth,
Our minds and hearts to bless—
Spontaneous wisdom breathed by health,
Truth breathed by cheerfulness.   20

One impulse from a vernal wood
May teach you more of man,
Of moral evil and of good,
Than all the sages can.

Sweet is the lore which Nature brings;   25
Our meddling intellect
Mis-shapes the beauteous forms of things:—
We murder to dissect.

Enough of Science and of Art;
Close up those barren leaves;   30
Come forth, and bring with you a heart
That watches and receives.

Lines Written in Early Spring

Written 1798

I HEARD a thousand blended notes,
While in a grove I sate reclined,
In that sweet mood when pleasant thoughts
Bring sad thoughts to the mind.

To her fair works did Nature link   5
The human soul that through me ran;
And much it grieved my heart to think
What man has made of man.

Through primrose tufts, in that green bower,
The periwinkle trailed its wreaths;   10
And 'tis my faith that every flower
Enjoys the air it breathes.

The birds around me hopped and played,
Their thoughts I cannot measure:—
But the least motion which they made,   15
It seemed a thrill of pleasure.

The budding twigs spread out their fan,
To catch the breezy air;
And I must think, do all I can,
That there was pleasure there.   20

If this belief from heaven be sent,
If such be Nature's holy plan,
Have I not reason to lament
What man has made of man?

To my Sister

Written 1798

IT is the first mild day of March:
Each minute sweeter than before,
The redbreast sings from the tall larch
That stands beside our door.

There is a blessing in the air,   5
Which seems a sense of joy to yield
To the bare trees, and mountains bare,
And grass in the green field.

My sister! ('tis a wish of mine)
Now that our morning meal is done,   10
Make haste, your morning task resign;
Come forth and feel the sun.

Edward will come with you;—and, pray,
Put on with speed your woodland dress;
And bring no book; for this one day   15
We'll give to idleness.

No joyless forms shall regulate
Our living calendar:
We from to-day, my Friend, will date
The opening of the year.   20

Love, now a universal birth,
From heart to heart is stealing,
From earth to man, from man to earth:
—It is the hour of feeling.

One moment now may give us more   25
Than years of toiling reason:
Our minds shall drink at every pore
The spirit of the season.

Some silent laws our hearts will make,
Which they shall long obey: 30
We for the year to come may take
Our temper from to-day.

And from the blessed power that rolls
About, below, above,
We'll frame the measure of our souls: 35
They shall be tuned to love.

Then come, my Sister! come, I pray,
With speed put on your woodland dress;
And bring no book: for this one day
We'll give to idleness.   40

The Last of the Flock

Written 1798

I

In distant countries have I been,
And yet I have not often seen
A healthy man, a man full grown,
Weep in the public roads, alone.
But such a one, on English ground,   5
And in the broad highway, I met;
Along the broad highway he came,
His cheeks with tears were wet:
Sturdy he seemed, though he was sad;
And in his arms a Lamb he had.   10

II

He saw me, and he turned aside,
As if he wished himself to hide:
And with his coat did then essay
To wipe those briny tears away.
I followed him, and said, 'My Friend,   15
What ails you? wherefore weep you so?'
—'Shame on me, Sir! this lusty Lamb,
He makes my tears to flow.
To-day I fetched him from the rock;
He is the last of all my flock.   20

III

'When I was young, a single man,
And after youthful follies ran,

Though little given to care and thought,
Yet, so it was, an ewe I bought;
And other sheep from her I raised,   25
As healthy sheep as you might see;
And then I married, and was rich
As I could wish to be;
Of sheep I numbered a full score,
And every year increased my store.   30

IV

'Year after year my stock it grew;
And from this one, this single ewe,
Full fifty comely sheep I raised,
As fine a flock as ever grazed!
Upon the Quantock hills they fed;   35
They throve, and we at home did thrive:
—This lusty Lamb of all my store
Is all that is alive;
And now I care not if we die,
And perish all of poverty.   40

V

'Six Children, Sir! had I to feed;
Hard labour in a time of need!
My pride was tamed, and in our grief
I of the Parish asked relief.
They said, I was a wealthy man;   45
My sheep upon the uplands fed,
And it was fit that thence I took
Whereof to buy us bread.
"Do this: how can we give to you,"
They cried, "what to the poor is due?"   50

VI

'I sold a sheep, as they had said,
And bought my little children bread,
And they were healthy with their food;
For me—it never did me good.
A woeful time it was for me,   55
To see the end of all my gains,
The pretty flock which I had reared
With all my care and pains,
To see it melt like snow away—
For me it was a woeful day.   60

VII

'Another still! and still another!
A little lamb, and then its mother!
It was a vein that never stopped—
Like blood-drops from my heart they dropped.
Till thirty were not left alive   65
They dwindled, dwindled, one by one;
And I may say, that many a time
I wished they all were gone—
Reckless of what might come at last
Were but the bitter struggle past.   70

VIII

'To wicked deeds I was inclined,
And wicked fancies crossed my mind;
And every man I chanced to see,
I thought he knew some ill of me:
No peace, no comfort could I find,   75
No ease, within doors or without;

And crazily and wearily
I went my work about;
And oft was moved to flee from home,
And hide my head where wild beasts roam.   80

IX

'Sir! 'twas a precious flock to me,
As dear as my own children be;
For daily with my growing store
I loved my children more and more.
Alas! it was an evil time;   85
God cursed me in my sore distress;
I prayed, yet every day I thought
I loved my children less;
And every week, and every day,
My flock it seemed to melt away.   90

X

'They dwindled, Sir, sad sight to see!
From ten to five, from five to three,
A lamb, a wether, and a ewe;—
And then at last from three to two;
And, of my fifty, yesterday   95
I had but only one:
And here it lies upon my arm,
Alas! and I have none;—
To-day I fetched it from the rock;
It is the last of all my flock.'   100

Her Eyes are Wild

Written 1798

I

HER eyes are wild, her head is bare,
The sun has burnt her coal-black hair;
Her eyebrows have a rusty stain,
And she came far from over the main.
She has a baby on her arm,   5
Or else she were alone:
And underneath the hay-stack warm,
And on the greenwood stone,
She talked and sung the woods among,
And it was in the English tongue.   10

II

'Sweet babe! they say that I am mad,
But nay, my heart is far too glad;
And I am happy when I sing
Full many a sad and doleful thing:
Then, lovely baby, do not fear!   15
I pray thee have no fear of me;
But safe as in a cradle, here
My lovely baby! thou shalt be:
To thee I know too much I owe;
I cannot work thee any woe.   20

III

'A fire was once within my brain;
And in my head a dull, dull pain;
And fiendish faces, one, two, three,
Hung at my breast, and pulled at me;

But then there came a sight of joy;   25
It came at once to do me good;
I waked, and saw my little boy,
My little boy of flesh and blood;
Oh joy for me that sight to see!
For he was here, and only he.   30

IV

'Suck, little babe, oh suck again!
It cools my blood; it cools my brain;
Thy lips I feel them, baby! they
Draw from my heart the pain away.
Oh! press me with thy little hand;   35
It loosens something at my chest;
About that tight and deadly band
I feel thy little fingers prest.
The breeze I see is in the tree:
It comes to cool my babe and me.   40

V

'Oh! love me, love me, little boy!
Thou art thy mother's only joy;
And do not dread the waves below,
When o'er the sea-rock's edge we go;
The high crag cannot work me harm,   45
Nor leaping torrents when they howl;
The babe I carry on my arm,
He saves for me my precious soul;
Then happy lie; for blest am I;
Without me my sweet babe would die.   50

VI

'Then do not fear, my boy! for thee
Bold as a lion will I be;

And I will always be thy guide,
Through hollow snows and rivers wide.
I'll build an Indian bower; I know   55
The leaves that make the softest bed:
And if from me thou wilt not go,
But still be true till I am dead,
My pretty thing! then thou shalt sing
As merry as the birds in spring.   60

VII

'Thy father cares not for my breast,
'Tis thine, sweet baby, there to rest;
'Tis all thine own!—and if its hue
Be changed, that was so fair to view,
'Tis fair enough for thee, my dove!   65
My beauty, little child, is flown,
But thou wilt live with me in love;
And what if my poor cheek be brown?
'Tis well for me, thou canst not see
How pale and wan it else would be.   70

VIII

'Dread not their taunts, my little Life;
I am thy father's wedded wife;
And underneath the spreading tree
We two will live in honesty.
If his sweet boy he could forsake,   75
With me he never would have stayed:
From him no harm my babe can take;
But he, poor man! is wretched made;
And every day we two will pray
For him that's gone and far away.   80

IX

'I'll teach my boy the sweetest things:
I'll teach him how the owlet sings.
My little babe! thy lips are still,
And thou hast almost sucked thy fill.
—Where art thou gone, my own dear child?   85
What wicked looks are those I see?
Alas! alas! that look so wild,
It never, never came from me:
If thou art mad, my pretty lad,
Then I must be for ever sad.   90

X

'Oh! smile on me, my little lamb!
For I thy own dear mother am:
My love for thee has well been tried:
I've sought thy father far and wide.
I know the poisons of the shade;   95
I know the earth-nuts fit for food:
Then, pretty dear, be not afraid:
We'll find thy father in the wood.
Now laugh and be gay, to the woods away!
And there, my babe, we'll live for aye.'   100

Lines

COMPOSED A FEW MILES ABOVE TINTERN ABBEY, ON
REVISITING THE BANKS OF THE WYE DURING A TOUR.
JULY 13, 1798

Written 1798

FIVE years have past; five summers, with the length
Of five long winters! and again I hear
These waters, rolling from their mountain-springs
With a soft inland murmur.[1]—Once again
Do I behold these steep and lofty cliffs,   5
That on a wild secluded scene impress
Thoughts of more deep seclusion; and connect
The landscape with the quiet of the sky.
The day is come when I again repose
Here, under this dark sycamore, and view   10
These plots of cottage-ground, these orchard-tufts,
Which at this season, with their unripe fruits,
Are clad in one green hue, and lose themselves
'Mid groves and copses. Once again I see
These hedge-rows, hardly hedge-rows, little lines   15
Of sportive wood run wild: these pastoral farms,
Green to the very door; and wreaths of smoke
Sent up, in silence, from among the trees!
With some uncertain notice, as might seem
Of vagrant dwellers in the houseless woods,   20
Or of some Hermit's cave, where by his fire
The Hermit sits alone.
                              These beauteous forms,
Through a long absence, have not been to me

[1] The river is not affected by the tides a few miles above Tintern.

As is a landscape to a blind man's eye:
But oft, in lonely rooms, and 'mid the din   25
Of towns and cities, I have owed to them
In hours of weariness, sensations sweet,
Felt in the blood, and felt along the heart;
And passing even into my purer mind,
With tranquil restoration:—feelings too   30
Of unremembered pleasure: such, perhaps,
As have no slight or trivial influence
On that best portion of a good man's life,
His little, nameless, unremembered, acts
Of kindness and of love. Nor less, I trust,   35
To them I may have owed another gift,
Of aspect more sublime; that blessed mood
In which the burthen of the mystery,
In which the heavy and the weary weight
Of all this unintelligible world,   40
Is lightened:—that serene and blessed mood,
In which the affections gently lead us on,—
Until, the breath of this corporeal frame
And even the motion of our human blood
Almost suspended, we are laid asleep   45
In body, and become a living soul:
While with an eye made quiet by the power
Of harmony, and the deep power of joy,
We see into the life of things.
                    If this
Be but a vain belief, yet, oh! how oft—   50
In darkness and amid the many shapes
Of joyless daylight; when the fretful stir
Unprofitable, and the fever of the world,
Have hung upon the beatings of my heart—
How oft, in spirit, have I turned to thee,   55

O sylvan Wye! thou wanderer thro' the woods,
How often has my spirit turned to thee!

   And now, with gleams of half-extinguished thought,
With many recognitions dim and faint,
And somewhat of a sad perplexity,   60
The picture of the mind revives again:
While here I stand, not only with the sense
Of present pleasure, but with pleasing thoughts
That in this moment there is life and food
For future years. And so I dare to hope,   65
Though changed, no doubt, from what I was when first
I came among these hills; when like a roe
I bounded o'er the mountains, by the sides
Of the deep rivers, and the lonely streams,
Wherever nature led: more like a man   70
Flying from something that he dreads than one
Who sought the thing he loved. For nature then
(The coarser pleasures of my boyish days,
And their glad animal movements all gone by)
To me was all in all.—I cannot paint   75
What then I was. The sounding cataract
Haunted me like a passion: the tall rock,
The mountain, and the deep and gloomy wood,
Their colours and their forms, were then to me
An appetite; a feeling and a love,   80
That had no need of a remoter charm,
By thought supplied nor any interest
Unborrowed from the eye.—That time is past,
And all its aching joys are now no more,
And all its dizzy raptures. Not for this   85
Faint I, nor mourn nor murmur; other gifts
Have followed; for such loss, I would believe,

Abundant recompense. For I have learned
To look on nature, not as in the hour
Of thoughtless youth; but hearing oftentimes   90
The still, sad music of humanity,
Nor harsh nor grating, though of ample power
To chasten and subdue. And I have felt
A presence that disturbs me with the joy
Of elevated thoughts; a sense sublime   95
Of something far more deeply interfused,
Whose dwelling is the light of setting suns,
And the round ocean and the living air,
And the blue sky, and in the mind of man:
A motion and a spirit, that impels   100
All thinking things, all objects of all thought,
And rolls through all things. Therefore am I still
A lover of the meadows and the woods,
And mountains; and of all that we behold
From this green earth; of all the mighty world   105
Of eye, and ear,—both what they half create,[1]
And what perceive; well pleased to recognise
In nature and the language of the sense
The anchor of my purest thoughts, the nurse,
The guide, the guardian of my heart, and soul   110
Of all my moral being.
                         Nor perchance,
If I were not thus taught, should I the more
Suffer my genial spirits to decay:
For thou art with me here upon the banks
Of this fair river; thou my dearest Friend,   115
My dear, dear Friend; and in thy voice I catch
The language of my former heart, and read

[1] This line has a close resemblance to an admirable line of Young's, the exact
expression of which I do not recollect.

My former pleasures in the shooting lights
Of thy wild eyes. Oh! yet a little while
May I behold in thee what I was once,   120
My dear, dear Sister! and this prayer I make,
Knowing that Nature never did betray
The heart that loved her; 'tis her privilege,
Through all the years of this our life, to lead
From joy to joy: for she can so inform   125
The mind that is within us, so impress
With quietness and beauty, and so feed
With lofty thoughts, that neither evil tongues,
Rash judgments, nor the sneers of selfish men,
Nor greetings where no kindness is, nor all   130
The dreary intercourse of daily life,
Shall e'er prevail against us, or disturb
Our cheerful faith, that all which we behold
Is full of blessings. Therefore let the moon
Shine on thee in thy solitary walk;   135
And let the misty mountain-winds be free
To blow against thee: and, in after years,
When these wild ecstasies shall be matured
Into a sober pleasure; when thy mind
Shall be a mansion for all lovely forms,   140
Thy memory be as a dwelling-place
For all sweet sounds and harmonies; oh! then,
If solitude, or fear, or pain, or grief,
Should be thy portion, with what healing thoughts
Of tender joy wilt thou remember me   145
And these my exhortations! Nor, perchance—
If I should be where I no more can hear
Thy voice, nor catch from thy wild eyes these gleams
Of past existence—wilt thou then forget
That on the banks of this delightful stream   150

We stood together; and that I, so long
A worshipper of Nature, hither came
Unwearied in that service: rather say
With warmer love—oh! with far deeper zeal
Of holier love. Nor wilt thou then forget,   155
That after many wanderings, many years
Of absence, these steep woods and lofty cliffs,
And this green pastoral landscape, were to me   gain.
More dear, both for themselves and for thy sake!

There was a Boy

Written 1798

THERE was a Boy; ye knew him well, ye cliffs
And islands of Winander!—many a time,
At evening, when the earliest stars began
To move along the edges of the hills,
Rising or setting, would he stand alone,   5
Beneath the trees, or by the glimmering lake;
And there, with fingers interwoven, both hands
Pressed closely palm to palm and to his mouth
Uplifted, he, as through an instrument,
Blew mimic hootings to the silent owls,   10
That they might answer him.—And they would shout
Across the watery vale, and shout again,
Responsive to his call,—with quivering peals,
And long halloos, and screams, and echoes loud
Redoubled and redoubled; concourse wild   15
Of jocund din! And, when there came a pause
Of silence such as baffled his best skill:
Then, sometimes, in that silence, while he hung
Listening, a gentle shock of mild surprise
Has carried far into his heart the voice   20
Of mountain-torrents; or the visible scene

Would enter unawares into his mind
With all its solemn imagery, its rocks,
Its woods, and that uncertain heaven received
Into the bosom of the steady lake.   25
    This boy was taken from his mates, and died
In childhood, ere he was full twelve years old.
Pre-eminent in beauty is the vale
Where he was born and bred: the church-yard hangs
Upon a slope above the village-school;   30
And, through that churchyard when my way has led
On summer-evenings, I believe, that there
A long half-hour together I have stood
Mute—looking at the grave in which he lies!

Nutting

Written 1798

————It seems a day
(I speak of one from many singled out)
One of those heavenly days that cannot die;
When, in the eagerness of boyish hope,
I left our cottage-threshold, sallying forth   5
With a huge wallet o'er my shoulders slung,
A nutting-crook in hand; and turned my steps
Tow'rd some far-distant wood, a Figure quaint,
Tricked out in proud disguise of cast-off weeds
Which for that service had been husbanded,   10
By exhortation of my frugal Dame—
Motley accoutrement, of power to smile
At thorns, and brakes, and brambles,—and, in truth,

More ragged than need was! O'er path-less rocks,
Through beds of matted fern, and tangled thickets,   15
Forcing my way, I came to one dear nook
Unvisited, where not a broken bough
Drooped with its withered leaves, ungracious sign
Of devastation; but the hazels rose
Tall and erect, with tempting clusters hung,   20
A virgin scene!—A little while I stood,
Breathing with such suppression of the heart
As joy delights in; and, with wise restraint
Voluptuous, fearless of a rival, eyed
The banquet;—or beneath the trees I sate   25
Among the flowers, and with the flowers I played;
A temper known to those who, after long
And weary expectation, have been blest
With sudden happiness beyond all hope.
Perhaps it was a bower beneath whose leaves   30
The violets of five seasons re-appear
And fade, unseen by any human eye;
Where fairy water-breaks do murmur on
For ever; and I saw the sparkling foam,
And—with my cheek on one of those green stones   35
That, fleeced with moss, under the shady trees,
Lay round me, scattered like a flock of sheep—
I heard the murmur and the murmuring sound,
In that sweet mood when pleasure loves to pay
Tribute to ease; and, of its joy secure,   40
The heart luxuriates with indifferent things,
Wasting its kindliness on stocks and stones,
And on the vacant air. Then up I rose,
And dragged to earth both branch and bough, with crash
And merciless ravage: and the shady nook   45
Of hazels, and the green and mossy bower,

Deformed and sullied, patiently gave up
Their quiet being: and, unless I now
Confound my present feelings with the past,
Ere from the mutilated bower I turned   50
Exulting, rich beyond the wealth of kings,
I felt a sense of pain when I beheld
The silent trees, and saw the intruding sky.—
Then, dearest Maiden, move along these shades
In gentleness of heart; with gentle hand   55
Touch—for there is a spirit in the woods.

Michael

A PASTORAL POEM

Written 1800

IF from the public way you turn your steps
Up the tumultuous brook of Green-head Ghyll,
You will suppose that with an upright path
Your feet must struggle; in such bold ascent,
The pastoral mountains front you, face to face.   5
But, courage! for around that boisterous brook
The mountains have all opened out themselves,
And made a hidden valley of their own.
No habitation can be seen; but they
Who journey thither find themselves alone   10
With a few sheep, with rocks and stones, and kites
That overhead are sailing in the sky.
It is in truth an utter solitude;
Nor should I have made mention of this Dell
But for one object which you might pass by,   15

Might see and notice not. Beside the brook
Appears a straggling heap of unhewn stones!
And to that simple object appertains
A story—unenriched with strange events,
Yet not unfit, I deem, for the fireside, 20
Or for the summer shade. It was the first
Of those domestic tales that spake to me
Of Shepherds, dwellers in the valleys, men
Whom I already loved;—not verily
For their own sakes, but for the fields and hills 25
Where was their occupation and abode.
And hence this Tale, while I was yet a Boy
Careless of books, yet having felt the power
Of Nature, by the gentle agency
Of natural objects, led me on to feel 30
For passions that were not my own, and think
(At random and imperfectly indeed)
On man, the heart of man, and human life.
Therefore, although it be a history
Homely and rude, I will relate the same 35
For the delight of a few natural hearts;
And, with yet fonder feeling, for the sake
Of youthful Poets, who among these hills
Will be my second self when I am gone.

  Upon the forest-side in Grasmere Vale 40
There dwelt a Shepherd, Michael was his name;
An old man, stout of heart, and strong of limb.
His bodily frame had been from youth to age
Of an unusual strength: his mind was keen,
Intense, and frugal, apt for all affairs, 45
And in his shepherd's calling he was prompt
And watchful more than ordinary men.
Hence had he learned the meaning of all winds,

Of blasts of every tone; and oftentimes,
When others heeded not, He heard the South   50
Make subterraneous music, like the noise
Of bagpipers on distant Highland hills.
The Shepherd, at such warning, of his flock
Bethought him, and he to himself would say,
'The winds are now devising work for me!'   55
And, truly, at all times, the storm, that drives
The traveller to a shelter, summoned him
Up to the mountains: he had been alone
Amid the heart of many thousand mists,
That came to him, and left him, on the heights.   60
So lived he till his eightieth year was past.
And grossly that man errs, who would suppose
That the green valleys, and the streams and rocks,
Were things indifferent to the Shepherd's thoughts.
Fields, where with cheerful spirits he had breathed   65
The common air; hills, which with vigorous step
He had so often climbed; which had impressed
So many incidents upon his mind
Of hardship, skill or courage, joy or fear;
Which, like a book, preserved the memory   70
Of the dumb animals, whom he had saved,
Had fed or sheltered, linking to such acts
The certainty of honourable gain;
Those fields, those hills—what could they less? had laid
Strong hold on his affections, were to him   75
A pleasurable feeling of blind love,
The pleasure which there is in life itself.
    His days had not been passed in singleness.
His Helpmate was a comely matron, old—
Though younger than himself full twenty years.   80
She was a woman of a stirring life,

Whose heart was in her house: two wheels she had
Of antique form; this large, for spinning wool;
That small, for flax; and if one wheel had rest,
It was because the other was at work.   85
The Pair had but one inmate in their house,
An only Child, who had been born to them
When Michael, telling o'er his years, began
To deem that he was old,—in shepherd's phrase,
With one foot in the grave. This only Son,   90
With two brave sheep-dogs tried in many a storm,
The one of an inestimable worth,
Made all their household. I may truly say,
That they were as a proverb in the vale
For endless industry. When day was gone,   95
And from their occupations out of doors
The Son and Father were come home, even then,
Their labour did not cease; unless when all
Turned to the cleanly supper-board, and there,
Each with a mess of pottage and skimmed milk,   100
Sat round the basket piled with oaten cakes,
And their plain home-made cheese. Yet when the meal
Was ended, Luke (for so the Son was named)
And his old Father both betook themselves
To such convenient work as might employ   105
Their hands by the fire-side; perhaps to card
Wool for the Housewife's spindle, or repair
Some injury done to sickle, flail, or scythe,
Or other implement of house or field.
      Down from the ceiling, by the chimney's edge,   110
That in our ancient uncouth country style
With huge and black projection overbrowed
Large space beneath, as duly as the light
Of day grew dim the Housewife hung a lamp;

An aged utensil, which had performed   115
Service beyond all others of its kind.
Early at evening did it burn—and late,
Surviving comrade of uncounted hours,
Which, going by from year to year, had found,
And left the couple neither gay perhaps   120
Nor cheerful, yet with objects and with hopes,
Living a life of eager industry.
And now, when Luke had reached his eighteenth year,
There by the light of this old lamp they sate,
Father and Son, while far into the night   125
The Housewife plied her own peculiar work,
Making the cottage through the silent hours
Murmur as with the sound of summer flies.
This light was famous in its neighbourhood,
And was a public symbol of the life   130
That thrifty Pair had lived. For, as it chanced,
Their cottage on a plot of rising ground
Stood single, with large prospect, north and south,
High into Easedale, up to Dunmail-Raise,
And westward to the village near the lake;   135
And from this constant light, so regular,
And so far seen, the House itself, by all
Who dwelt within the limits of the vale,
Both old and young, was named THE EVENING STAR.
     Thus living on through such a length of years,   140
The Shepherd, if he loved himself, must needs
Have loved his Helpmate; but to Michael's heart
This son of his old age was yet more dear—
Less from instinctive tenderness, the same
Fond spirit that blindly works in the blood of all— 145
Than that a child, more than all other gifts
That earth can offer to declining man,

Brings hope with it, and forward-looking thoughts,
And stirrings of inquietude, when they
By tendency of nature needs must fail.   150
Exceeding was the love he bare to him,
His heart and his heart's joy! For often-times
Old Michael, while he was a babe in arms,
Had done him female service, not alone
For pastime and delight, as is the use   155
Of fathers, but with patient mind enforced
To acts of tenderness; and he had rocked
His cradle, as with a woman's gentle hand.
　And in a later time, ere yet the Boy
Had put on boy's attire, did Michael love,   160
Albeit of a stern unbending mind,
To have the Young-one in his sight, when he
Wrought in the field, or on his shepherd's stool
Sate with a fettered sheep before him stretched
Under the large old oak, that near his door   165
Stood single, and, from matchless depth of shade,
Chosen for the Shearer's covert from the sun,
Thence in our rustic dialect was called
The CLIPPING TREE,[1] a name which yet it bears.
There, while they two were sitting in the shade,   170
With others round them, earnest all and blithe,
Would Michael exercise his heart with looks
Of fond correction and reproof bestowed
Upon the Child, if he disturbed the sheep
By catching at their legs, or with his shouts   175
Scared them, while they lay still beneath the shears.
　And when by Heaven's good grace the boy grew up
A healthy Lad, and carried in his cheek
Two steady roses that were five years old;

[1] Clipping is the word used in the North of England for shearing.

Then Michael from a winter coppice cut   180
With his own hand a sapling, which he hooped
With iron, making it throughout in all
Due requisites a perfect shepherd's staff,
And gave it to the Boy; wherewith equipt
He as a watchman oftentimes was placed   185
At gate or gap, to stem or turn the flock;
And, to his office prematurely called,
There stood the urchin, as you will divine,
Something between a hindrance and a help;
And for this cause not always, I believe,   190
Receiving from his Father hire of praise;
Though nought was left undone which staff, or voice,
Or looks, or threatening gestures, could perform.

   But soon as Luke, full ten years old, could stand
Against the mountain blasts; and to the heights,   195
Not fearing toil, nor length of weary ways,
He with his Father daily went, and they
Were as companions, why should I relate
That objects which the Shepherd loved before
Were dearer now? that from the Boy there came   200
Feelings and emanations—things which were
Light to the sun and music to the wind;
And that the old Man's heart seemed born again?

   Thus in his Father's sight the Boy grew up:
And now, when he had reached his eighteenth year,   205
He was his comfort and his daily hope.

   While in this sort the simple household lived
From day to day, to Michael's ear there came
Distressful tidings. Long before the time
Of which I speak, the Shepherd had been bound   210
In surety for his brother's son, a man
Of an industrious life, and ample means;

But unforeseen misfortunes suddenly
Had prest upon him; and old Michael now
Was summoned to discharge the forfeiture,   215
A grievous penalty, but little less
Than half his substance. This unlooked-for claim,
At the first hearing, for a moment took
More hope out of his life than he supposed
That any old man ever could have lost.   220
As soon as he had armed himself with strength
To look his trouble in the face, it seemed
The Shepherd's sole resource to sell at once
A portion of his patrimonial fields.
Such was his first resolve; he thought again,   225
And his heart failed him. 'Isabel,' said he,
Two evenings after he had heard the news,
'I have been toiling more than seventy years,
And in the open sunshine of God's love
Have we all lived; yet if these fields of ours   230
Should pass into a stranger's hand, I think
That I could not lie quiet in my grave.
Our lot is a hard lot; the sun himself
Has scarcely been more diligent than I;
And I have lived to be a fool at last   235
To my own family. An evil man
That was, and made an evil choice, if he
Were false to us; and, if he were not false,
There are ten thousand to whom loss like this
Had been no sorrow. I forgive him;—but   240
'Twere better to be dumb than to talk thus.

   'When I began, my purpose was to speak
Of remedies and of a cheerful hope.
Our Luke shall leave us, Isabel; the land
Shall not go from us, and it shall be free;   245

He shall possess it, free as is the wind
That passes over it. We have, thou know'st,
Another kinsman—he will be our friend
In this distress. He is a prosperous man,
Thriving in trade—and Luke to him shall go,   250
And with his kinsman's help and his own thrift
He quickly will repair this loss, and then
He may return to us. If here he stay,
What can be gained? Where every one is poor,
What can be done?'

                  At this the old Man paused,   255
And Isabel sat silent, for her mind
Was busy, looking back into past times.
There's Richard Bateman, thought she to herself,
He was a parish-boy—at the church-door
They made a gathering for him, shillings, pence,   260
And halfpennies, wherewith the neighbours bought
A basket, which they filled with pedlar's wares;
And, with this basket on his arm, the lad
Went up to London, found a master there,
Who, out of many, chose the trusty boy   265
To go and overlook his merchandise
Beyond the seas; where he grew wondrous rich,
And left estates and monies to the poor,
And, at his birth-place, built a chapel floored
With marble, which he sent from foreign lands.   270
These thoughts, and many others of like sort,
Passed quickly through the mind of Isabel,
And her face brightened. The old Man was glad,
And thus resumed:—'Well, Isabel! this scheme
These two days has been meat and drink to me.   275
Far more than we have lost is left us yet.
—We have enough—I wish indeed that I

Were younger;—but this hope is a good hope.
Make ready Luke's best garments, of the best
Buy for him more, and let us send him forth   280
To-morrow, or the next day, or to-night:
—If he *could* go, the Boy should go to-night.'

    Here Michael ceased, and to the fields went forth
With a light heart. The Housewife for five days
Was restless morn and night, and all day long   285
Wrought on with her best fingers to prepare
Things needful for the journey of her son.
But Isabel was glad when Sunday came
To stop her in her work: for, when she lay
By Michael's side, she through the last two nights   290
Heard him, how he was troubled in his sleep:
And when they rose at morning she could see
That all his hopes were gone. That day at noon
She said to Luke, while they two by themselves
Were sitting at the door, 'Thou must not go: 295
We have no other Child but thee to lose,
None to remember—do not go away,
For if thou leave thy Father he will die.'
The Youth made answer with a jocund voice;
And Isabel, when she had told her fears,   300
Recovered heart. That evening her best fare
Did she bring forth, and all together sat
Like happy people round a Christmas fire.

    With daylight Isabel resumed her work;
And all the ensuing week the house appeared   305
As cheerful as a grove in Spring: at length
The expected letter from their kinsman came,
With kind assurances that he would do
His utmost for the welfare of the Boy;
To which, requests were added, that forthwith   310

He might be sent to him. Ten times or more
The letter was read over; Isabel
Went forth to show it to the neighbours round;
Nor was there at that time on English land
A prouder heart than Luke's. When Isabel   315
Had to her house returned, the old Man said,
'He shall depart to-morrow.' To this word
The Housewife answered, talking much of things
Which, if at such short notice he should go,
Would surely be forgotten. But at length   320
She gave consent, and Michael was at ease.

   Near the tumultuous brook of Green-head Ghyll,
In that deep valley, Michael had designed
To build a Sheep-fold; and, before he heard
The tidings of his melancholy loss,   325
For this same purpose he had gathered up
A heap of stones, which by the streamlet's edge
Lay thrown together, ready for the work.
With Luke that evening thitherward he walked:
And soon as they had reached the place he stopped,   330
And thus the old Man spake to him:—'My son,
To-morrow thou wilt leave me: with full heart
I look upon thee, for thou art the same
That wert a promise to me ere thy birth,
And all thy life hast been my daily joy.   335
I will relate to thee some little part
Of our two histories; 'twill do thee good
When thou art from me, even if I should touch
On things thou canst not know of.——After thou
First cam'st into the world—as oft befalls   340
To new-born infants—thou didst sleep away
Two days, and blessings from thy Father's tongue
Then fell upon thee. Day by day passed on,

And still I loved thee with increasing love.
Never to living ear came sweeter sounds   345
Than when I heard thee by our own fire-side
First uttering, without words, a natural tune;
While thou, a feeding babe, didst in thy joy
Sing at thy Mother's breast. Month followed month,
And in the open fields my life was passed   350
And on the mountains; else I think that thou
Hadst been brought up upon thy Father's knees.
But we were playmates, Luke: among these hills,
As well thou knowest, in us the old and young
Have played together, nor with me didst thou   355
Lack any pleasure which a boy can know.'
Luke had a manly heart; but at these words
He sobbed aloud. The old Man grasped his hand,
And said, 'Nay, do not take it so—I see
That these are things of which I need not speak.   360
—Even to the utmost I have been to thee
A kind and a good Father: and herein
I but repay a gift which I myself
Received at others' hands; for, though now old
Beyond the common life of man, I still   365
Remember them who loved me in my youth.
Both of them sleep together: there they lived,
As all their Forefathers had done; and when
At length their time was come, they were not loth
To give their bodies to the family mould.   370
I wished that thou should'st live the life they lived,
But 'tis a long time to look back, my Son,
And see so little gain from threescore years.
These fields were burthened when they came to me;
Till I was forty years of age, not more   375
Than half of my inheritance was mine.

I toiled and toiled; God blessed me in my work,
And till these three weeks past the land was free.
—It looks as if it never could endure
Another Master. Heaven forgive me, Luke,   380
If I judge ill for thee, but it seems good
That thou shouldst go.'
                                At this the old Man paused;
Then, pointing to the stones near which they stood,
Thus, after a short silence, he resumed:
'This was a work for us; and now, my Son,   385
It is a work for me. But, lay one stone—
Here, lay it for me, Luke, with thine own hands.
Nay, Boy, be of good hope;—we both may live
To see a better day. At eighty-four
I still am strong and hale;—do thou thy part;   390
I will do mine.—I will begin again
With many tasks that were resigned to thee:
Up to the heights, and in among the storms,
Will I without thee go again, and do
All works which I was wont to do alone,   395
Before I knew thy face.—Heaven bless thee, Boy!
Thy heart these two weeks has been beating fast
With many hopes; it should be so—yes—yes—
I knew that thou couldst never have a wish
To leave me, Luke: thou hast been bound to me   400
Only by links of love: when thou art gone,
What will be left to us!—But I forget
My purposes. Lay now the corner-stone,
As I requested; and hereafter, Luke,
When thou art gone away, should evil men   405
Be thy companions, think of me, my Son,
And of this moment; hither turn thy thoughts,
And God will strengthen thee: amid all fear

And all temptation, Luke, I pray that thou
May'st bear in mind the life thy Fathers lived,   410
Who, being innocent, did for that cause
Bestir them in good deeds. Now, fare thee well—
When thou return'st, thou in this place wilt see
A work which is not here: a covenant
'Twill be between us; but, whatever fate   415
Befall thee, I shall love thee to the last,
And bear thy memory with me to the grave.'
    The Shepherd ended here; and Luke stooped down,
And, as his Father had requested, laid
The first stone of the Sheep-fold. At the sight   420
The old Man's grief broke from him; to his heart
He pressed his Son, he kissèd him and wept;
And to the house together they returned.
—Hushed was that House in peace, or seeming peace,
Ere the night fell:—with morrow's dawn the Boy   425
Began his journey, and when he had reached
The public way, he put on a bold face;
And all the neighbours, as he passed their doors,
Came forth with wishes and with farewell prayers,
That followed him till he was out of sight.   430
    A good report did from their Kinsman come,
Of Luke and his well-doing: and the Boy
Wrote loving letters, full of wondrous news,
Which, as the Housewife phrased it, were throughout
'The prettiest letters that were ever seen.'   435
Both parents read them with rejoicing hearts.
So, many months passed on: and once again
The Shepherd went about his daily work
With confident and cheerful thoughts; and now
Sometimes when he could find a leisure hour   440
He to that valley took his way, and there

Wrought at the Sheep-fold. Meantime Luke began
To slacken in his duty; and, at length,
He in the dissolute city gave himself
To evil courses: ignominy and shame   445
Fell on him, so that he was driven at last
To seek a hiding-place beyond the seas.
X There is a comfort in the strength of love; X
'Twill make a thing endurable, which else
Would overset the brain, or break the heart: 450
I have conversed with more than one who well
Remember the old Man, and what he was
Years after he had heard this heavy news.
His bodily frame had been from youth to age
Of an unusual strength. Among the rocks   455
He went, and still looked up to sun and cloud,
And listened to the wind; and, as before,
Performed all kinds of labour for his sheep,
And for the land, his small inheritance.
And to that hollow dell from time to time   460
Did he repair, to build the Fold of which
His flock had need. 'Tis not forgotten yet
The pity which was then in every heart
For the old Man—and 'tis believed by all
That many and many a day he thither went,   465
And never lifted up a single stone.

   There, by the Sheep-fold, sometimes was he seen
Sitting alone, or with his faithful Dog,
Then old, beside him, lying at his feet.
The length of full seven years, from time to time,   470
He at the building of this Sheep-fold wrought,
And left the work unfinished when he died.
Three years, or little more, did Isabel
Survive her Husband: at her death the estate

Was sold, and went into a stranger's hand.   475
The Cottage which was named the EVENING STAR
Is gone—the ploughshare has been through the ground
On which it stood; great changes have been wrought
In all the neighbourhood:—yet the oak is left
That grew beside their door; and the remains   480
Of the unfinished Sheep-fold may be seen
Beside the boisterous brook of Green-head Ghyll.

The Reverie of Poor Susan

Written 1797

AT the corner of Wood Street, when daylight appears,
Hangs a Thrush that sings loud, it has sung for three years:
Poor Susan has passed by the spot, and has heard
In the silence of morning the song of the Bird.

'Tis a note of enchantment; what ails her? She sees   5
A mountain ascending, a vision of trees;
Bright volumes of vapour through Lothbury glide,
And a river flows on through the vale of Cheapside.

Green pastures she views in the midst of the dale,
Down which she so often has tripped with her pail;   10
And a single small cottage, a nest like a dove's,
The one only dwelling on earth that she loves.

She looks, and her heart is in heaven: but they fade,
The mist and the river, the hill and the shade:
The stream will not flow, and the hill will not rise,   15
And the colours have all passed away from her eyes!

Written 1799

THREE years she grew in sun and shower,
Then Nature said, 'A lovelier flower
On earth was never sown;
This Child I to myself will take;
She shall be mine, and I will make   5
A Lady of my own.

'Myself will to my darling be
Both law and impulse: and with me
The Girl, in rock and plain,
In earth and heaven, in glade and bower,   10
Shall feel an overseeing power
To kindle or restrain.

'She shall be sportive as the fawn
That wild with glee across the lawn
Or up the mountain springs;   15
And her's shall be the breathing balm,
And her's the silence and the calm
Of mute insensate things.

'The floating clouds their state shall lend
To her; for her the willow bend;   20
Nor shall she fail to see
Even in the motions of the Storm
Grace that shall mould the Maiden's form
By silent sympathy.

'The stars of midnight shall be dear   25
To her; and she shall lean her ear
In many a secret place

Where rivulets dance their wayward round,
And beauty born of murmuring sound
Shall pass into her face.   30

'And vital feelings of delight
Shall rear her form to stately height,
Her virgin bosom swell;
Such thoughts to Lucy I will give
While she and I together live   35
Here in this happy dell.'

Thus Nature spake—The work was done—
How soon my Lucy's race was run!
She died, and left to me
This heath, this calm, and quiet scene;   40
The memory of what has been,
And never more will be.

Written 1799

A SLUMBER did my spirit seal;
    I had no human fears:
She seemed a thing that could not feel
    The touch of earthly years.

No motion has she now, no force;   5
    She neither hears nor sees;
Rolled round in earth's diurnal course,
    With rocks, and stones, and trees.

Written 1799

STRANGE fits of passion have I known:
And I will dare to tell,
But in the Lover's ear alone,
What once to me befell.

When she I loved looked every day   5
Fresh as a rose in June,
I to her cottage bent my way,
Beneath an evening-moon.

Upon the moon I fixed my eye,
All over the wide lea;   10
With quickening pace my horse drew nigh
Those paths so dear to me.

And now we reached the orchard-plot;
And, as we climbed the hill,
The sinking moon to Lucy's cot   15
Came near, and nearer still.

In one of those sweet dreams I slept,
Kind Nature's gentlest boon!
And all the while my eyes I kept
On the descending moon.   20

My horse moved on; hoof after hoof
He raised, and never stopped:
When down behind the cottage roof,
At once, the bright moon dropped.

What fond and wayward thoughts will slide   25
Into a Lover's head!
'O mercy!' to myself I cried,
'If Lucy should be dead!'

Written 1799

SHE dwelt among the untrodden ways
　　Beside the springs of Dove,
A Maid whom there were none to praise
　　And very few to love:

A violet by a mossy stone　　　　　　　　5
　　Half hidden from the eye!
—Fair as a star, when only one
　　Is shining in the sky.

She lived unknown, and few could know
　　When Lucy ceased to be;　　　　　　　10
But she is in her grave, and, oh,
　　The difference to me!

WITH SOME RELATED POEMS

Written 1801

I TRAVELLED among unknown men,
  In lands beyond the sea;
Nor, England! did I know till then
  What love I bore to thee.

'Tis past, that melancholy dream!   5
  Nor will I quit thy shore
A second time; for still I seem
  To love thee more and more.

Among thy mountains did I feel
  The joy of my desire;   10
And she I cherished turned her wheel
  Beside an English fire.

Thy mornings showed, thy nights concealed,
  The bowers where Lucy played;
And thine too is the last green field   15
  That Lucy's eyes surveyed.

The Sparrow's Nest

Written 1801

BEHOLD, within the leafy shade,
Those bright blue eggs together laid!
On me the chance-discovered sight
Gleamed like a vision of delight.
I started—seeming to espy   5
The home and sheltered bed,
The Sparrow's dwelling, which, hard by
My Father's house, in wet or dry
My sister Emmeline and I
    Together visited.   10

She looked at it and seemed to fear it;
Dreading, tho' wishing, to be near it:
Such heart was in her, being then
A little Prattler among men.
The Blessing of my later years   15
Was with me when a boy;
She gave me eyes, she gave me ears;
And humble cares, and delicate fears;
A heart, the fountain of sweet tears;
    And love, and thought, and joy.   20

Written 1804

SHE was a Phantom of delight
When first she gleamed upon my sight;
A lovely Apparition, sent
To be a moment's ornament;
Her eyes as stars of Twilight fair;
Like Twilight's, too, her dusky hair;

But all things else about her drawn
From May-time and the cheerful Dawn;
A dancing Shape, an Image gay,
To haunt, to startle, and way-lay.   10

I saw her upon nearer view,
A Spirit, yet a Woman too!
Her household motions light and free,
And steps of virgin-liberty;
A countenance in which did meet   15
Sweet records, promises as sweet;
A Creature not too bright or good
For human nature's daily food;
For transient sorrows, simple wiles,
Praise, blame, love, kisses, tears, and smiles.   20

And now I see with eye serene
The very pulse of the machine;
A Being breathing thoughtful breath,
A Traveller between life and death;
The reason firm, the temperate will,   25
Endurance, foresight, strength, and skill;
A perfect Woman, nobly planned,
To warn, to comfort, and command;
And yet a Spirit still, and bright
With something of angelic light.   30

The Sailor's Mother

Written 1802

ONE morning (raw it was and wet—
A foggy day in winter time)

A Woman on the road I met,
　Not old, though something past her prime:
　Majestic in her person, tall and straight;   5
And like a Roman matron's was her mien and gait.

　The ancient spirit is not dead;
　Old times, thought I, are breathing there;
　Proud was I that my country bred
　Such strength, a dignity so fair: 10
　She begged an alms, like one in poor estate;
I looked at her again, nor did my pride abate.

　When from these lofty thoughts I woke,
　'What is it,' said I, 'that you bear,
　Beneath the covert of your Cloak,   15
　Protected from this cold damp air?'
　She answered, soon as she the question heard,
'A simple burthen, Sir, a little Singing-bird.'

　And, thus continuing, she said,
　'I had a Son, who many a day   20
　Sailed on the seas, but he is dead;
　In Denmark he was cast away:
　And I have travelled weary miles to see
If aught which he had owned might still remain for me.

　'The bird and cage they both were his: 25
　'Twas my Son's bird; and neat and trim
　He kept it: many voyages
　The singing-bird had gone with him;
　When last he sailed, he left the bird behind;
From bodings, as might be, that hung upon his mind.   30

'He to a fellow-lodger's care
Had left it, to be watched and fed,
And pipe its song in safety;—there
I found it when my Son was dead;
And now, God help me for my little wit!   35
I bear it with me, Sir;—he took so much delight in it.'

Beggars

Written 1802

SHE had a tall man's height or more;
Her face from summer's noontide heat
No bonnet shaded, but she wore
A mantle, to her very feet
Descending with a graceful flow,   5
And on her head a cap as white as new-fallen snow.

Her skin was of Egyptian brown:
Haughty, as if her eye had seen
Its own light to a distance thrown,
She towered, fit person for a Queen   10
To lead those ancient Amazonian files;
Or ruling Bandit's wife among the Grecian isles.

Advancing, forth she stretched her hand
And begged an alms with doleful plea
That ceased not; on our English land   15
Such woes, I knew, could never be;
And yet a boon I gave her, for the creature
Was beautiful to see—a weed of glorious feature.

I left her, and pursued my way;
And soon before me did espy   20
A pair of little Boys at play,
Chasing a crimson butterfly;
The taller followed with his hat in hand,
Wreathed round with yellow flowers the gayest of the land.

The other wore a rimless crown   25
With leaves of laurel stuck about;
And while both followed up and down,
Each whooping with a merry shout,
In their fraternal features I could trace
Unquestionable lines of that wild Suppliant's face.   30

Yet *they*, so blithe of heart, seemed fit
For finest tasks of earth or air:
Wings let them have, and they might flit
Precursors to Aurora's car,
Scattering fresh flowers; though happier far, I ween,   35
To hunt their fluttering game o'er rock and level green.

They dart across my path—but lo,
Each ready with a plaintive whine!
Said I, 'not half an hour ago
Your Mother has had alms of mine.'   40
'That cannot be,' one answered—'she is dead:'—
I looked reproof—they saw—but neither hung his head.

'She has been dead, Sir, many a day.'—
'Hush, boys! you're telling me a lie;
It was your Mother, as I say!'   45
And, in the twinkling of an eye,
'Come! come!' cried one, and without more ado
Off to some other play the joyous Vagrants flew!

Resolution and Independence

Written 1802

I

THERE was a roaring in the wind all night;
The rain came heavily and fell in floods;
But now the sun is rising calm and bright;
The birds are singing in the distant woods;
Over his own sweet voice the Stock-dove broods;   5
The Jay makes answer as the Magpie chatters;
And all the air is filled with pleasant noise of waters.

II

All things that love the sun are out of doors;
The sky rejoices in the morning's birth;
The grass is bright with rain-drops;—on the moors   10
The hare is running races in her mirth;
And with her feet she from the plashy earth
Raises a mist; that, glittering in the sun,
Runs with her all the way, wherever she doth run.

III

I was a Traveller then upon the moor;   15
I saw the hare that raced about with joy;
I heard the woods and distant waters roar;
Or heard them not, as happy as a boy;
The pleasant season did my heart employ:
My old remembrances went from me wholly;   20
And all the ways of men, so vain and melancholy.

loss / power of mind ?

IV

But, as it sometimes chanceth, from the might
Of joy in minds that can no further go,
As high as we have mounted in delight
In our dejection do we sink as low;   25
To me that morning did it happen so;
And fears and fancies thick upon me came;
Dim sadness—and blind thoughts, I knew not, nor could name.

V

I heard the sky-lark warbling in the sky;
And I bethought me of the playful hare: 30
Even such a happy Child of earth am I;
Even as these blissful creatures do I fare;
Far from the world I walk, and from all care;
But there may come another day to me—
Solitude, pain of heart, distress, and poverty.   35

VI

My whole life I have lived in pleasant thought,
As if life's business were a summer mood;
As if all needful things would come unsought
To genial faith, still rich in genial good;
But how can He expect that others should   40
Build for him, sow for him, and at his call
Love him, who for himself will take no heed at all?

VII

I thought of Chatterton, the marvellous Boy,
The sleepless Soul that perished in his pride;
Of Him who walked in glory and in joy   45
Following his plough, along the mountain-side:

By our own spirits are we deified:
We Poets in our youth begin in gladness;
But thereof come in the end despondency and madness.

VIII

Now, whether it were by peculiar grace,   50
A leading from above, a something given,
Yet it befell that, in this lonely place,
When I with these untoward thoughts had striven,
Beside a pool bare to the eye of heaven
I saw a Man before me unawares: 55
The oldest man he seemed that ever wore grey hairs.

IX

As a huge stone is sometimes seen to lie
Couched on the bald top of an eminence;
Wonder to all who do the same espy,
By what means it could thither come, and whence;   60
So that it seems a thing endued with sense:
Like a sea-beast crawled forth, that on a shelf
Of rock or sand reposeth, there to sun itself;

X

Such seemed this Man, not all alive nor dead,
Nor all asleep—in his extreme old age: 65
His body was bent double, feet and head
Coming together in life's pilgrimage;
As if some dire constraint of pain, or rage
Of sickness felt by him in times long past,
A more than human weight upon his frame had cast.   70

XI

Himself he propped, limbs, body, and pale face,
Upon a long grey staff of shaven wood:
And, still as I drew near with gentle pace,
Upon the margin of that moorish flood
Motionless as a cloud the old Man stood,   75
That heareth not the loud winds when they call;
And moveth all together, if it move at all.

XII

At length, himself unsettling, he the pond
Stirred with his staff, and fixedly did look
Upon the muddy water, which he conned,   80
As if he had been reading in a book:
And now a stranger's privilege I took;
And, drawing to his side, to him did say,
'This morning give us promise of a glorious day.'

XIII

A gentle answer did the old Man make,   85
In courteous speech which forth he slowly drew:
And him with further words I thus bespake,
'What occupation do you there pursue?
This is a lonesome place for one like you.'
Ere he replied, a flash of mild surprise   90
Broke from the sable orbs of his yet-vivid eyes.

XIV

His words came feebly, from a feeble chest,
But each in solemn order followed each,
With something of a lofty utterance drest—

Choice word and measured phrase, above the reach   95
Of ordinary men; a stately speech;
Such as grave Livers do in Scotland use,
Religious men, who give to God and man their dues.

XV

He told, that to these waters he had come
To gather leeches, being old and poor: 100
Employment hazardous and wearisome!
And he had many hardships to endure:
From pond to pond he roamed, from moor to moor;
Housing, with God's good help, by choice or chance;
And in this way he gained an honest maintenance.   105

XVI

The old Man still stood talking by my side;
But now his voice to me was like a stream
Scarce heard; nor word from word could I divide;
And the whole body of the Man did seem
Like one whom I had met with in a dream;   110
Or like a man from some far region sent,
To give me human strength, by apt admonishment.

XVII

My former thoughts returned: the fear that kills;
And hope that is unwilling to be fed;
Cold, pain, and labour, and all fleshly ills;   115
And mighty Poets in their misery dead.
—Perplexed, and longing to be comforted,
My question eagerly did I renew,
'How is it that you live, and what is it you do?'

XVIII

He with a smile did then his words repeat;   120
And said that, gathering leeches, far and wide
He travelled; stirring thus about his feet
The waters of the pools where they abide.
'Once I could meet with them on every side;
But they have dwindled long by slow decay;   125
Yet still I persevere, and find them where I may.'

message –
gain of knowledge

XIX

While he was talking thus, the lonely place,
The old Man's shape, and speech—all troubled me:
In my mind's eye I seemed to see him pace
About the weary moors continually,   130
Wandering about alone and silently.
While I these thoughts within myself pursued,
He, having made a pause, the same discourse renewed.

XX

And soon with this he other matter blended,
Cheerfully uttered, with demeanour kind,   135
But stately in the main; and when he ended,
I could have laughed myself to scorn to find
In that decrepit Man so firm a mind.
'God,' said I, 'be my help and stay secure;
I'll think of the Leech-gatherer on the lonely moor!'   140

Miscellaneous Sonnets

Written ?

NUNS fret not at their convent's narrow room;
And hermits are contented with their cells;
And students with their pensive citadels;
Maids at the wheel, the weaver at his loom,
Sit blithe and happy; bees that soar for bloom,   5
High as the highest Peak of Furness-fells,
Will murmur by the hour in foxglove bells:
In truth the prison, unto which we doom
Ourselves, no prison is: and hence for me,
In sundry moods, 'twas pastime to be bound   10
Within the Sonnet's scanty plot of ground;
Pleased if some Souls (for such there needs must be)
Who have felt the weight of too much liberty,
Should find brief solace there, as I have found.

Written 1802

IT is a beauteous evening, calm and free,
The holy time is quiet as a Nun
Breathless with adoration; the broad sun
Is sinking down in its tranquillity;
The gentleness of heaven broods o'er the Sea: 5
Listen! the mighty Being is awake,
And doth with his eternal motion make
A sound like thunder—everlastingly.
Dear Child! dear Girl! that walkest with me here,
If thou appear untouched by solemn thought,   10

Thy nature is not therefore less divine:
Thou liest in Abraham's bosom all the year;
And worshipp'st at the Temple's inner shrine,
God being with thee when we know it not.

Written ?

THE world is too much with us; late and soon,
Getting and spending, we lay waste our powers:
Little we see in Nature that is ours;
We have given our hearts away, a sordid boon!
This Sea that bares her bosom to the moon;   5
The winds that will be howling at all hours,
And are up-gathered now like sleeping flowers;
For this, for everything, we are out of tune;
It moves us not.—Great God! I'd rather be
A Pagan suckled in a creed outworn;   10
So might I, standing on this pleasant lea,
Have glimpses that would make me less forlorn;
Have sight of Proteus rising from the sea;
Or hear old Triton blow his wreathèd horn.

Composed upon Westminster Bridge, September 3, 1802

Written 1802

EARTH has not anything to show more fair:
Dull would he be of soul who could pass by
A sight so touching in its majesty:
This City now doth, like a garment, wear
The beauty of the morning; silent, bare,   5

Ships, towers, domes, theatres, and temples lie
Open unto the fields, and to the sky;
All bright and glittering in the smokeless air.
Never did sun more beautifully steep
In his first splendour, valley, rock, or hill;   10
Ne'er saw I, never felt, a calm so deep!
The river glideth at his own sweet will:
Dear God! the very houses seem asleep;
And all that mighty heart is lying still!

Written ?. *Poems* (1827)

SCORN not the Sonnet; Critic, you have frowned,
Mindless of its just honours; with this key
Shakspeare unlocked his heart; the melody
Of this small lute gave ease to Petrarch's wound;
A thousand times this pipe did Tasso sound;   5
With it Camöens soothed an exile's grief;
The Sonnet glittered a gay myrtle leaf
Amid the cypress with which Dante crowned
His visionary brow: a glow-worm lamp,
It cheered mild Spenser, called from Faery-land   10
To struggle through dark ways; and, when a damp
Fell round the path of Milton, in his hand
The Thing became a trumpet; whence he blew
Soul-animating strains—alas, too few!

Written 1802

I WANDERED lonely as a cloud
That floats on high o'er vales and hills,
When all at once I saw a crowd,
A host, of golden daffodils;

Beside the lake, beneath the trees,　　　　5
Fluttering and dancing in the breeze.

Continuous as the stars that shine
And twinkle on the milky way,
They stretched in never-ending line
Along the margin of a bay:　　　　10
Ten thousand saw I at a glance,
Tossing their heads in sprightly dance.

The waves beside them danced; but they
Out-did the sparkling waves in glee:
A poet could not but be gay,　　　　15
In such a jocund company:
I gazed—and gazed—but little thought
What wealth the show to me had brought:

For oft, when on my couch I lie
In vacant or in pensive mood,　　　　20
They flash upon that inward eye
Which is the bliss of solitude;
And then my heart with pleasure fills,
And dances with the daffodils.

Written in March

WHILE RESTING ON THE BRIDGE AT THE FOOT OF BROTHER'S WATER

Written 1802

THE Cock is crowing,
The stream is flowing,
The small birds twitter,
The lake doth glitter,
The green field sleeps in the sun;　　　　5

The oldest and youngest
Are at work with the strongest;
The cattle are grazing,
Their heads never raising;
There are forty feeding like one!   10

Like an army defeated
The snow hath retreated,
And now doth fare ill
On the top of the bare hill;
The Ploughboy is whooping—anon—anon: 15
  There's joy in the mountains;
  There's life in the fountains;
  Small clouds are sailing,
  Blue sky prevailing;
The rain is over and gone!   20

To the Cuckoo

Written 1802

O BLITHE New-comer! I have heard,
I hear thee and rejoice.
O Cuckoo! shall I call thee Bird,
Or but a wandering Voice?

While I am lying on the grass   5
Thy twofold shout I hear,
From hill to hill it seems to pass
At once far off, and near.

Though babbling only to the Vale,
Of sunshine and of flowers,   10
Thou bringest unto me a tale
Of visionary hours.

Thrice welcome, darling of the Spring!
Even yet thou art to me
No bird, but an invisible thing,   15
A voice, a mystery;

The same whom in my schoolboy days
I listened to; that Cry
Which made me look a thousand ways
In bush, and tree, and sky.   20

To seek thee did I often rove
Through woods and on the green;
And thou wert still a hope, a love;
Still longed for, never seen.

And I can listen to thee yet;   25
Can lie upon the plain
And listen, till I do beget
That golden time again.

O blessèd Bird! the earth we pace
Again appears to be   30
An unsubstantial, faery place;
That is fit home for Thee!

From POEMS DEDICATED TO NATIONAL INDEPENDENCE AND LIBERTY

PART I

IV. 1801

Written 1802

I GRIEVED for Buonaparté, with a vain
And an unthinking grief! The tenderest mood
Of that Man's mind—what can it be? what food
Fed his first hopes? what knowledge could *he* gain?
'Tis not in battles that from youth we train   5
The Governor who must be wise and good,
And temper with the sternness of the brain
Thoughts motherly, and meek as womanhood.
Wisdom doth live with children round her knees:
Books, leisure, perfect freedom, and the talk   10
Man holds with week-day man in the hourly walk
Of the mind's business: these are the degrees
By which true Sway doth mount; this is the stalk
True Power doth grow on; and her rights are these.

VI. On the Extinction of the Venetian Republic

Written 1802

ONCE did She hold the gorgeous east in fee;
And was the safeguard of the west: the worth
Of Venice did not fall below her birth,

Venice, the eldest Child of Liberty.
She was a maiden City, bright and free;   5
No guile seduced, no force could violate;
And, when she took unto herself a Mate,
She must espouse the everlasting Sea.
And what if she had seen those glories fade,
Those titles vanish, and that strength decay;   10
Yet shall some tribute of regret be paid
When her long life hath reached its final day:
Men are we, and must grieve when even the Shade
Of that which once was great, is passed away.

VIII. To Toussaint L'Ouverture

Written 1802

TOUSSAINT, the most unhappy man of men!
Whether the whistling Rustic tend his plough
Within thy hearing, or thy head be now
Pillowed in some deep dungeon's earless den;—
O miserable Chieftain! where and when   5
Wilt thou find patience! Yet die not; do thou
Wear rather in thy bonds a cheerful brow:
Though fallen thyself, never to rise again,
Live, and take comfort. Thou hast left behind
Powers that will work for thee; air, earth, and skies;   10
There's not a breathing of the common wind
That will forget thee; thou hast great allies;
Thy friends are exultations, agonies,
And love, and man's unconquerable mind.

XII. Thought of a Briton on the Subjugation of Switzerland

Written 1806 or early in 1807

TWO Voices are there; one is of the sea,
One of the mountains; each a mighty Voice:
In both from age to age thou didst rejoice,
They were thy chosen music, Liberty!
There came a Tyrant, and with holy glee   5
Thou fought'st against him; but hast vainly striven:
Thou from thy Alpine holds at length art driven,
Where not a torrent murmurs heard by thee.
Of one deep bliss thine ear hath been bereft:
Then cleave, O cleave to that which still is left;   10
For, high-souled Maid, what sorrow would it be
That Mountain floods should thunder as before,
And Ocean bellow from his rocky shore,
And neither awful Voice be heard by thee!

XIV. London, 1802

Written 1802

MILTON! thou shouldst be living at this hour:
England hath need of thee: she is a fen
Of stagnant waters: altar, sword, and pen,
Fireside, the heroic wealth of hall and bower,
Have forfeited their ancient English dower   5
Of inward happiness. We are selfish men;
Oh! raise us up, return to us again;
And give us manners, virtue, freedom, power.

Thy soul was like a Star, and dwelt apart;
Thou hadst a voice whose sound was like the sea: 10
Pure as the naked heavens, majestic, free,
So didst thou travel on life's common way,
In cheerful godliness; and yet thy heart
The lowliest duties on herself did lay.

XVI

Written 1802 or 1803

IT is not to be thought of that the Flood
Of British freedom, which, to the open sea
Of the world's praise, from dark antiquity
Hath flowed, 'with pomp of waters, unwithstood,'
Roused though it be full often to a mood   5
Which spurns the check of salutary bands,
That this most famous Stream in bogs and sands
Should perish; and to evil and to good
Be lost for ever. In our halls is hung
Armoury of the invincible Knights of old: 10
We must be free or die, who speak the tongue
That Shakespeare spake; the faith and morals hold
Which Milton held.—In every thing we are sprung
Of Earth's first blood, have titles manifold.

XX. October, 1803

THESE times strike monied worldlings with dismay:
Even rich men, brave by nature, taint the air
With words of apprehension and despair:

While tens of thousands, thinking on the affray,
Men unto whom sufficient for the day   5
And minds not stinted or untilled are given,
Sound, healthy, children of the God of heaven,
Are cheerful as the rising sun in May.
What do we gather hence but firmer faith
That every gift of noble origin   10
Is breathed upon by Hope's perpetual breath;
That virtue and the faculties within
Are vital,—and that riches are akin
To fear, to change, to cowardice, and death?

XXI

Written probably 1803

ENGLAND! the time is come when thou should'st wean
Thy heart from its emasculating food:
The truth should now be better understood;
Old things have been unsettled; we have seen
Fair seed-time, better harvest might have been   5
But for thy trespasses; and, at this day,
If for Greece, Egypt, India, Africa,
Aught good were destined, thou would'st step between.
England! all nations in this charge agree:
But worse, more ignorant in love and hate,   10
Far—far more abject, is thine Enemy:
Therefore the wise pray for thee, though the freight
Of thy offences be a heavy weight:
Oh grief that Earth's best hopes rest all with Thee!

PART II

XXVII. Indignation of a High-minded Spaniard

1810

Written 1810. *Poems* (1815)

WE can endure that He should waste our lands,
Despoil our temples, and by sword and flame
Return us to the dust from which we came;
Such food a Tyrant's appetite demands:
And we can brook the thought that by his hands   5
Spain may be overpowered, and he possess,
For his delight, a solemn wilderness
Where all the brave lie dead. But, when of bands
Which he will break for us he dares to speak,
Of benefits, and of a future day   10
When our enlightened minds shall bless his sway;
Then, the strained heart of fortitude proves weak;
Our groans, our blushes, our pale cheeks declare
That he has power to inflict what we lack strength to bear.

Lines

Composed at Grasmere, during a walk one Evening, after a stormy day, the Author having just read in a Newspaper that the dissolution of Mr. Fox was hourly expected.
Written 1806

LOUD is the Vale! the Voice is up
With which she speaks when storms are gone,
A mighty unison of streams!
Of all her Voices, One!

Loud is the Vale;—this inland Depth   5
In peace is roaring like the Sea;
Yon star upon the mountain-top
Is listening quietly.

Sad was I, even to pain deprest,
Importunate and heavy load![1]   10
The Comforter hath found me here,
Upon this lonely road;

And many thousands now are sad—
Wait the fulfilment of their fear;
For he must die who is their stay   15
Their glory disappear.

A Power is passing from the earth
To breathless Nature's dark abyss;
But when the great and good depart
What is it more than this—   20

That Man, who is from God sent forth,
Doth yet again to God return?—
Such ebb and flow must ever be,
Then wherefore should we mourn?

[1] *Importuna e grave salma.*—Michael Angelo.

Yarrow Unvisited

Written 1803

See the various Poems the scene of which is laid upon the banks of the Yarrow;
in particular, the exquisite Ballad of Hamilton beginning—

'Busk ye, busk ye, my bonny, bonny Bride,
Busk ye, busk ye, my winsome Marrow!'

FROM Stirling castle we had seen
The mazy Forth unravelled;
Had trod the banks of Clyde, and Tay,
And with the Tweed had travelled;
And when we came to Clovenford,   5
Then said my '*winsome Marrow*,'
'Whate'er betide, we'll turn aside,
And see the Braes of Yarrow.'

'Let Yarrow folk, *frae* Selkirk town,
Who have been buying, selling,   10
Go back to Yarrow, 'tis their own;
Each maiden to her dwelling!
On Yarrow's banks let herons feed,
Hares couch, and rabbits burrow!
But we will downward with the Tweed,   15
Nor turn aside to Yarrow.

'There's Galla Water, Leader Haughs,
Both lying right before us;
And Dryborough, where with chiming Tweed
The lintwhites sing in chorus;   20
There's pleasant Tiviot-dale, a land
Made blithe with plough and harrow:
Why throw away a needful day
To go in search of Yarrow?

'What's Yarrow but a river bare,   25
That glides the dark hills under?
There are a thousand such elsewhere
As worthy of your wonder.'
—Strange words they seemed of slight and scorn;
My True-love sighed for sorrow;   30
And looked me in the face, to think
I thus could speak of Yarrow!

'Oh! green,' said I, 'are Yarrow's holms,
And sweet is Yarrow flowing!
Fair hangs the apple frae the rock,[1]   35
But we will leave it growing.
O'er hilly path, and open Strath,
We'll wander Scotland thorough;
But, though so near, we will not turn
Into the dale of Yarrow.   40

'Let beeves and home-bred kine partake
The sweets of Burn-mill meadow;
The swan on still St. Mary's Lake
Float double, swan and shadow!
We will not see them; will not go,   45
To-day, nor yet to-morrow;
Enough if in our hearts we know
There's such a place as Yarrow.

'Be Yarrow stream unseen, unknown!
It must, or we shall rue it: 50
We have a vision of our own;
Ah! why should we undo it?
The treasured dreams of times long past,
We'll keep them, winsome Marrow!

[1] See Hamilton's Ballad as above.

For when we're there, although 'tis fair,   55
  'Twill be another Yarrow!

'If Care with freezing years should come,
And wandering seem but folly,—
Should we be loth to stir from home,
And yet be melancholy;   60
Should life be dull, and spirits low,
'Twill soothe us in our sorrow,
That earth hath something yet to show,
The bonny holms of Yarrow!'

Stepping Westward

Written 1805

While my Fellow-traveller and I were walking by the side of Loch Ketterine,
  one fine evening after sunset, in our road to a Hut where, in the course of
  our Tour, we had been hospitably entertained some weeks before, we met, in
  one of the loneliest parts of that solitary region, two well-dressed Women,
  one of whom said to us, by way of greeting, 'What, you are stepping
  westward?'

'*WHAT, you are stepping westward?*'—'*Yea.*'
—'Twould be a *wildish* destiny,
If we, who thus together roam
In a strange Land, and far from home,
Were in this place the guests of Chance: 5
Yet who would stop, or fear to advance,
Though home or shelter he had none,
With such a sky to lead him on?

The dewy ground was dark and cold;
Behind, all gloomy to behold;   10
And stepping westward seemed to be
A kind of *heavenly* destiny:

I liked the greeting; 'twas a sound
Of something without place or bound;
And seemed to give me spiritual right   15
To travel through that region bright.

The voice was soft, and she who spake
Was walking by her native lake:
The salutation had to me
The very sound of courtesy: 20
Its power was felt; and while my eye
Was fixed upon the glowing Sky,
The echo of the voice enwrought
A human sweetness with the thought
Of travelling through the world that lay   25
Before me in my endless way.

The Solitary Reaper

Written 1805

BEHOLD her, single in the field,
Yon solitary Highland Lass!
Reaping and singing by herself;
Stop here, or gently pass!
Alone she cuts and binds the grain,   5
And sings a melancholy strain;
O listen! for the Vale profound
Is overflowing with the sound.

No Nightingale did ever chaunt
More welcome notes to weary bands   10
Of travellers in some shady haunt,
Among Arabian sands:

A voice so thrilling ne'er was heard
In spring-time from the Cuckoo-bird,
Breaking the silence of the seas   15
Among the farthest Hebrides.

Will no one tell me what she sings?—
Perhaps the plaintive numbers flow
For old, unhappy, far-off things,
And battles long ago: 20
Or is it some more humble lay,
Familiar matter of to-day?
Some natural sorrow, loss, or pain,
That has been, and may be again?

Whate'er the theme, the Maiden sang   25
As if her song could have no ending;
I saw her singing at her work,
And o'er the sickle bending:—
I listened, motionless and still;
And, as I mounted up the hill,   30
The music in my heart I bore,
Long after it was heard no more.

Yarrow Visited

SEPTEMBER, 1814

Poems (1815)

AND is this—Yarrow?—*This* the Stream
Of which my fancy cherished,
So faithfully, a waking dream?
An image that hath perished!

O that some Minstrel's harp were near,   5
To utter notes of gladness,
And chase this silence from the air,
That fills my heart with sadness!

Yet why?—a silvery current flows
With uncontrolled meanderings;   10
Nor have these eyes by greener hills
Been soothed, in all my wanderings.
And, through her depths, Saint Mary's Lake
Is visibly delighted;
For not a feature of those hills   15
Is in the mirror slighted.

A blue sky bends o'er Yarrow vale,
Save where that pearly whiteness
Is round the rising sun diffused,
A tender hazy brightness;   20
Mild dawn of promise! that excludes
All profitless dejection;
Though not unwilling here to admit
A pensive recollection.

Where was it that the famous Flower   25
Of Yarrow Vale lay bleeding?
His bed perchance was yon smooth mound
On which the herd is feeding:
And haply from this crystal pool,
Now peaceful as the morning,   30
The Water-wraith ascended thrice—
And gave his doleful warning.

Delicious is the Lay that sings
The haunts of happy Lovers,

The path that leads them to the grove,   35
The leafy grove that covers:
And Pity sanctifies the Verse
That paints, by strength of sorrow,
The unconquerable strength of love;
Bear witness, rueful Yarrow!   40

But thou, that didst appear so fair
To fond imagination,
Dost rival in the light of day
Her delicate creation:
Meek loveliness is round thee spread,   45
A softness still and holy;
The grace of forest charms decayed,
And pastoral melancholy.

That region left, the vale unfolds
Rich groves of lofty stature,   50
With Yarrow winding through the pomp
Of cultivated nature;
And, rising from those lofty groves,
Behold a Ruin hoary!
The shattered front of Newark's Towers,   55
Renowned in Border story.

Fair scenes for childhood's opening bloom,
For sportive youth to stray in;
For manhood to enjoy his strength;
And age to wear away in!   60
Yon cottage seems a bower of bliss,
A covert for protection
Of tender thoughts, that nestle there—
The brood of chaste affection.

How sweet, on this autumnal day,   65
The wild-wood fruits to gather,
And on my True-love's forehead plant
A crest of blooming heather!
And what if I enwreathed my own!
'Twere no offence to reason;   70
The sober Hills thus deck their brows
To meet the wintry season.

I see—but not by sight alone,
Loved Yarrow, have I won thee;
A ray of fancy still survives—   75
Her sunshine plays upon thee!
Thy ever-youthful waters keep
A course of lively pleasure;
And gladsome notes by lips can breathe,
Accordant to the measure.   80

The vapours linger round the Heights,
They melt, and soon must vanish;
One hour is theirs, nor more is mine—
Sad thought, which I would banish,
But that I know, where'er I go,   85
Thy genuine image, Yarrow!
Will dwell with me—to heighten joy,
And cheer my mind in sorrow.

Song at the Feast of Brougham Castle

UPON THE RESTORATION OF LORD CLIFFORD, THE
SHEPHERD, TO THE ESTATES AND HONOURS OF HIS
ANCESTORS

Written 1807

HIGH in the breathless Hall the Minstrel sate,
And Emont's murmur mingled with the Song.—
The words of ancient time I thus translate,
A festal strain that hath been silent long:—

'From town to town, from tower to tower,   5
The red rose is a gladsome flower.
Her thirty years of winter past,
The red rose is revived at last;
She lifts her head for endless spring,
For everlasting blossoming: 10
Both roses flourish, red and white:
In love and sisterly delight
The two that were at strife are blended,
And all old troubles now are ended.—
Joy! joy to both! but most to her   15
Who is the flower of Lancaster!
Behold her how She smiles to-day
On this great throng, this bright array!
Fair greeting doth she send to all
From every corner of the hall;   20
But chiefly from above the board
Where sits in state our rightful Lord,
A Clifford to his own restored!

'They came with banner, spear, and shield;
And it was proved in Bosworth-field.   25
Not long the Avenger was withstood—
Earth helped him with the cry of blood:
St. George was for us, and the might
Of blessed Angels crowned the right.
Loud voice the Land has uttered forth,   30
We loudest in the faithful north:
Our fields rejoice, our mountains ring,
Our streams proclaim a welcoming;
Our strong-abodes and castles see
The glory of their loyalty.   35

'How glad is Skipton at this hour—
Though lonely, a deserted Tower;
Knight, squire, and yeoman, page and groom:
We have them at the feast of Brough'm.
How glad Pendragon—though the sleep   40
Of years be on her!—She shall reap
A taste of this great pleasure, viewing
As in a dream her own renewing.
Rejoiced is Brough, right glad, I deem,
Beside her little humble stream;   45
And she that keepeth watch and ward
Her statelier Eden's course to guard;
They both are happy at this hour,
Though each is but a lonely Tower:—
But here is perfect joy and pride   50
For one fair House by Emont's side,
This day, distinguished without peer,
To see her Master and to cheer—
Him, and his Lady-mother dear!

'Oh! it was a time forlorn   55
When the fatherless was born—
Give her wings that she may fly,
Or she sees her infant die!
Swords that are with slaughter wild
Hunt the Mother and the Child.   60
Who will take them from the light?
—Yonder is a man in sight—
Yonder is a house—but where?
No, they must not enter there.
To the caves, and to the brooks,   65
To the clouds of heaven she looks;
She is speechless, but her eyes
Pray in ghostly agonies.
Blissful Mary, Mother mild,
Maid and Mother undefiled,   70
Save a Mother and her Child!

'Now Who is he that bounds with joy
On Carrock's side, a Shepherd-boy?
No thoughts hath he but thoughts that pass
Light as the wind along the grass.   75
Can this be He who hither came
In secret, like a smothered flame?
O'er whom such thankful tears were shed
For shelter, and a poor man's bread!
God loves the Child; and God hath willed   80
That those dear words should be fulfilled,
The Lady's words, when forced away
The last she to her Babe did say:
"My own, my own, thy Fellow-guest
I may not be; but rest thee, rest,   85
For lowly shepherd's life is best!"

'Alas! when evil men are strong
No life is good, no pleasure long.
The Boy must part from Mosedale's groves,
And leave Blencathara's rugged coves,   90
And quit the flowers that summer brings
To Glenderamakin's lofty springs;
Must vanish, and his careless cheer
Be turned to heaviness and fear.
—Give Sir Lancelot Threlkeld praise!   95
Hear it, good man, old in days!
Thou tree of covert and of rest
For this your Bird that is distrest;
Among thy branches safe he lay,
And he was free to sport and play,   100
When falcons were abroad for prey.

'A recreant harp, that sings of fear
And heaviness in Clifford's ear!
I said, when evil men are strong,
No life is good, no pleasure long,   105
A weak and cowardly untruth!
Our Clifford was a happy Youth,
And thankful through a weary time,
That brought him up to manhood's prime.
—Again he wanders forth at will,   110
And tends a flock from hill to hill:
His garb is humble; ne'er was seen
Such garb with such a noble mien;
Among the shepherd-grooms no mate
Hath he, a Child of strength and state!   115
Yet lacks not friends for simple glee,
Nor yet for higher sympathy.
To his side the fallow-deer

Came, and rested without fear;
The eagle, lord of land and sea,   120
Stooped down to pay him fealty;
And both the undying fish that swim
Through Bowscale-tarn did wait on him;
The pair were servants of his eye
In their immortality;   125
And glancing, gleaming, dark or bright,
Moved to and fro, for his delight.
He knew the rocks which Angels haunt
Upon the mountains visitant;
He hath kenned them taking wing: 130
And into caves where Faeries sing
He hath entered; and been told
By Voices how men lived of old.
Among the heavens his eye can see
The face of thing that is to be;   135
And, if that men report him right,
His tongue could whisper words of might.
—Now another day is come,
Fitter hope, and nobler doom;
He hath thrown aside his crook,   140
And hath buried deep his book;
Armour rusting in his halls
On the blood of Clifford calls;—
"Quell the Scot," exclaims the Lance—
Bear me to the heart of France,   145
Is the longing of the Shield—
Tell thy name, thou trembling Field;
Field of death, where'er thou be,
Groan thou with our victory!
Happy day, and mighty hour,   150
When our Shepherd in his power,

Mailed and horsed, with lance and sword,
To his ancestors restored
Like a re-appearing Star,
Like a glory from afar,   155
First shall head the flock of war!'

Alas! the impassioned minstrel did not know
How, by Heaven's grace, this Clifford's heart was framed:
How he, long forced in humble walks to go,
Was softened into feeling, soothed, and tamed.   160

Love had he found in huts where poor men lie;
His daily teachers had been woods and rills,
The silence that is in the starry sky,
The sleep that is among the lonely hills.

In him the savage virtue of the Race,   165
Revenge, and all ferocious thoughts were dead:
Nor did he change; but kept in lofty place
The wisdom which adversity had bred.

Glad were the vales, and every cottage hearth;
The Shepherd-lord was honoured more and more;   170
And, ages after he was laid in earth,
'The good Lord Clifford' was the name he bore.

Yew-Trees

Written 1803 (?). *Poems* (1815)

THERE is a Yew-tree, pride of Lorton Vale,
Which to this day stands single, in the midst
Of its own darkness, as it stood of yore:

Not loth to furnish weapons for the bands
Of Umfraville or Percy ere they marched   5
To Scotland's heaths; or those that crossed the sea
And drew their sounding bows at Azincour,
Perhaps at earlier Crecy, or Poictiers.
Of vast circumference and gloom profound
This solitary Tree! a living thing   10
Produced too slowly ever to decay;
Of form and aspect too magnificent
To be destroyed. But worthier still of note
Are those fraternal Four of Borrowdale,
Joined in one solemn and capacious grove;   15
Huge trunks! and each particular trunk a growth
Of intertwisted fibres serpentine
Up-coiling, and inveterately convolved;
Nor uninformed with Phantasy, and looks
That threaten the profane;—a pillared shade,   20
Upon whose grassless floor of red-brown hue,
By sheddings from the pining umbrage tinged
Perennially—beneath whose sable roof
Of boughs, as if for festal purpose decked
With unrejoicing berries—ghostly Shapes   25
May meet at noontide; Fear and trembling Hope,
Silence and Foresight; Death the Skeleton
And Time the Shadow;—there to celebrate,
As in a natural temple scattered o'er
With altars undisturbed of mossy stone,   30
United worship; or in mute repose
To lie, and listen to the mountain flood
Murmuring from Glaramara's inmost caves.

Written 1802

My heart leaps up when I behold
   A rainbow in the sky:
So was it when my life began;
So is it now I am a man;
So be it when I sh~~~   5
   Or l~
Th~

[handwritten marginalia, partly obscured by a paper slip:] Immortality   rhythmic hip with er line in poem.

Ode: Intir
Recollec

The ~~~~~~~~~~ ~~e Man;
And ~~~~ ~~~~ my days to be
Bound each to each by natural piety.

Written 1802–1804

I

There was a time when meadow, grove, and stream,
The earth, and every common sight,
   To me did seem
   Apparelled in celestial light,
The glory and the freshness of a dream.   *loss*   5
It is not now as it hath been of yore;—
   Turn wheresoe'er I may,
    By night or day,
The things which I have seen I now can see no more.

II

The Rainbow comes and goes,   10
And lovely is the Rose,
The Moon doth with delight
Look round her when the heavens are bare;
Waters on a starry night
Are beautiful and fair;   15
The sunshine is a glorious birth;
But yet I know, where'er I go,
That there hath past away a glory from the earth.

III

Now, while the birds thus sing a joyous song,
And while the young lambs bound   20
As to the tabor's sound,
To me alone there came a thought of grief:
A timely utterance gave that thought relief,
And I again am strong:
The cataracts blow their trumpets from the steep;   25
No more shall grief of mine the season wrong;
I hear the Echoes through the mountains throng,
The Winds come to me from the fields of sleep,
And all the earth is gay;
Land and sea   30
Give themselves up to jollity,
And with the heart of May
Doth every Beast keep holiday;—
Thou Child of Joy,
Shout round me, let me hear thy shouts, thou happy
Shepherd-boy!   35

IV

Ye blessèd Creatures, I have heard the call
  Ye to each other make; I see
The heavens laugh with you in your jubilee;
  My heart is at your festival,
    My head hath its coronal,   40
The fulness of your bliss, I feel—I feel it all.
      Oh evil day! if I were sullen
      While Earth herself is adorning,
        This sweet May-morning,
      And the Children are culling   45
        On every side,
      In a thousand valleys far and wide,
      Fresh flowers; while the sun shines warm,
And the Babe leaps up on his Mother's arm:—
      I hear, I hear, with joy I hear!   50
      —But there's a Tree, of many, one,
A single Field which I have looked upon,
Both of them speak of something that is gone:
      The Pansy at my feet
      Doth the same tale repeat: 55
Whither is fled the visionary gleam?
Where is it now, the glory and the dream?

V

Our birth is but a sleep and a forgetting:
The Soul that rises with us, our life's Star,
      Hath had elsewhere its setting,   60
        And cometh from afar:
      Not in entire forgetfulness,
      And not in utter nakedness,
But trailing clouds of glory do we come
      From God, who is our home: 65

Heaven lies about us in our infancy!
Shades of the prison-house begin to close   *loss of freedom?*
    Upon the growing Boy,
      But He
Beholds the light, and whence it flows,   70
    He sees it in his joy;
The Youth, who daily farther from the east
    Must travel, still is Nature's Priest,
    And by the vision splendid
    Is on his way attended;   75
At length the Man perceives it die away,
And fade into the light of common day.

VI

foster mother.

Earth fills her lap with pleasures of her own;
Yearnings she hath in her own natural kind,
And, even with something of a Mother's mind,   80
    And no unworthy aim,
    The homely Nurse doth all she can
To make her Foster-child, her Inmate Man,
    Forget the glories he hath known,
And that imperial palace whence he came.   85

VII

Behold the Child among his new-born blisses,
A six years' Darling of a pigmy size!
See, where 'mid work of his own hand he lies,
Fretted by sallies of his mother's kisses,
With light upon him from his father's eyes!   90
See, at his feet, some little plan or chart,
Some fragment from his dream of human life,
Shaped by himself with newly-learned art;

  A wedding or a festival,
  A mourning or a funeral;
    And this hath now his heart,   95
    And unto this he frames his song:
      Then will he fit his tongue
To dialogues of business, love, or strife;
    But it will not be long   100
    Ere this be thrown aside,
    And with new joy and pride
The little Actor cons another part;
Filling from time to time his 'humorous stage'
With all the Persons, down to palsied Age,   105
That Life brings with her in her equipage;
    As if his whole vocation
    Were endless imitation.

VIII

Thou, whose exterior semblance doth belie
    Thy Soul's immensity;   110
Thou best Philosopher, who yet dost keep
Thy heritage, thou Eye among the blind,
That, deaf and silent, read'st the eternal deep,
Haunted for ever by the eternal mind,—
    Mighty Prophet! Seer blest!   115
    On whom those truths do rest,
Which we are toiling all our lives to find,
In darkness lost, the darkness of the grave;
Thou, over whom thy Immortality
Broods like the Day, a Master o'er a Slave,   120
A Presence which is not to be put by;
Thou little Child, yet glorious in the might
Of heaven-born freedom on thy being's height,

Why with such earnest pains dost thou provoke
The years to bring the inevitable yoke,   125
Thus blindly with thy blessedness at strife?
Full soon thy Soul shall have her earthly freight,
And custom lie upon thee with a weight,
Heavy as frost, and deep almost as life!

                                    IX

          O joy! that in our embers   130
          Is something that doth live,
          That nature yet remembers
          What was so fugitive!
The thought of our past years in me doth breed
Perpetual benediction: not indeed   135
For that which is most worthy to be blest;
Delight and liberty, the simple creed
Of Childhood, whether busy or at rest,
With new-fledged hope still fluttering in his breast:—
             Not for these I raise   140
             The song of thanks and praise;
          But for those obstinate questionings
          Of sense and outward things,
          Fallings from us, vanishings;
          Blank misgivings of a Creature   145
Moving about in worlds not realised,
High instincts before which our mortal Nature
Did tremble like a guilty Thing surprised:
             But for those first affections,
             Those shadowy recollections,   150
          Which, be they what they may,
Are yet the fountain light of all our day,
Are yet a master light of all our seeing;

Uphold us, cherish, and have power to make
Our noisy years seem moments in the being 155
Of the eternal Silence: truths that wake,
       To perish never;
Which neither listlessness, nor mad endeavour,
       Nor Man nor Boy,
Nor all that is at enmity with joy, 160
Can utterly abolish or destroy!
       Hence in a season of calm weather
       Though inland far we be,
Our Souls have sight of that immortal sea
       Which brought us hither, 165
       Can in a moment travel thither,
And see the Children sport upon the shore,
And hear the mighty waters rolling evermore.

X

Then sing, ye Birds, sing, sing a joyous song!
       And let the young Lambs bound 170
       As to the tabor's sound!
We in thought will join your throng,
       Ye that pipe and ye that play,
       Ye that through your hearts to-day
       Feel the gladness of the May! 175
What though the radiance which was once so bright
Be now for ever taken from my sight,
       Though nothing can bring back the hour
Of splendour in the grass, of glory in the flower;
       We will grieve not, rather find 180
       Strength in what remains behind;
       In the primal sympathy
       Which having been must ever be;

In the soothing thoughts that spring
   Out of human suffering;   185
   In the faith that looks through death,
In years that bring the philosophic mind.

XI

And O, ye Fountains, Meadows, Hills, and Groves,
Forebode not any severing of our loves!
Yet in my heart of hearts I feel your might;   190
I only have relinquished one delight
To live beneath your more habitual sway.
I love the Brooks which down their channels fret,
Even more than when I tripped lightly as they;
The innocent brightness of a new-born Day   195
     Is lovely yet;
The Clouds that gather round the setting sun
Do take a sober colouring from an eye
That hath kept watch o'er man's mortality;
Another race hath been, and other palms are won.   200
Thanks to the human heart by which we live,
Thanks to its tenderness, its joys, and fears,
To me the meanest flower that blows can give
Thoughts that do often lie too deep for tears.

Ode to Duty

Written 1804

'Jam non consilio bonus, sed more eò perductus, ut non tantum
rectè facere possim, sed nisi rectè facere non possim.'

STERN Daughter of the Voice of God!
O Duty! If that name thou love
Who art a light to guide, a rod
To check the erring, and reprove;

Thou, who art victory and law   5
When empty terrors overawe;
From vain temptations dost set free;
And calm'st the weary strife of frail humanity!

There are who ask not if thine eye
Be on them; who, in love and truth,   10
Where no misgiving is, rely
Upon the genial sense of youth;
Glad Hearts! without reproach or blot;
Who do thy work, and know it not:
Oh! if through confidence misplaced   15
They fail, thy saving arms, dread Power! around them cast.

Serene will be our days and bright,
And happy will our nature be,
When love is an unerring light,
And joy its own security.   20
And they a blissful course may hold
Even now, who, not unwisely bold,
Live in the spirit of this creed;
Yet seek thy firm support, according to their need.

I, loving freedom, and untried;   25
No sport of every random gust,
Yet being to myself a guide,
Too blindly have reposed my trust:
And oft, when in my heart was heard
Thy timely mandate, I deferred   30
The task, in smoother walks to stray;
But thee I now would serve more strictly, if I may.

Through no disturbance of my soul,
Or strong compunction in me wrought,
I supplicate for thy control;   35
But in the quietness of thought:

Me this unchartered freedom tires;
I feel the weight of chance-desires:
My hopes no more must change their name,
I long for a repose that ever is the same.   40

[Yet not the less would I throughout
Still act according to the voice
Of my own wish; and feel past doubt
That my submissiveness was choice:
Not seeking in the school of pride   45
For 'precepts over dignified',
Denial and restraint I prize
No farther than they breed a second Will more wise.]

Stern Lawgiver! yet thou dost wear
The Godhead's most benignant grace;   50
Nor know we anything so fair
As is the smile upon thy face:
Flowers laugh before thee on their beds
And fragrance in thy footing treads;
Thou dost preserve the stars from wrong;   55
And the most ancient heavens, through Thee, are fresh
      and strong.

To humbler functions, awful Power!
I call thee: I myself commend
Unto thy guidance from this hour;
Oh, let my weakness have an end!   60
Give unto me, made lowly wise,
The spirit of self-sacrifice;
The confidence of reason give;
And in the light of truth thy Bondman let me live!

Elegiac Stanzas

SUGGESTED BY A PICTURE OF PEELE CASTLE, IN A STORM, PAINTED BY SIR GEORGE BEAUMONT

Written 1805

I WAS thy neighbour once, thou rugged Pile!
Four summer weeks I dwelt in sight of thee:
I saw thee every day; and all the while
Thy Form was sleeping on a glassy sea.

So pure the sky, so quiet was the air!   5
So like, so very like, was day to day!
Whene'er I looked, thy Image still was there;
It trembled, but it never passed away.

How perfect was the calm! it seemed no sleep;
No mood, which season takes away, or brings: 10
I could have fancied that the mighty Deep
Was even the gentlest of all gentle Things.

Ah! THEN, if mine had been the Painter's hand,
To express what then I saw; and add the gleam,
The light that never was, on sea or land,   15
The consecration, and the Poet's dream;

I would have planted thee, thou hoary Pile
Amid a world how different from this!
Beside a sea that could not cease to smile;
On tranquil land, beneath a sky of bliss.   20

Thou shouldst have seemed a treasure-house divine
Of peaceful years; a chronicle of heaven;—
Of all the sunbeams that did ever shine
The very sweetest had to thee been given.

A Picture had it been of lasting ease,   25
Elysian quiet, without toil or strife;
No motion but the moving tide, a breeze,
Or merely silent Nature's breathing life.

Such, in the fond illusion of my heart,
Such Picture would I at that time have made: 30
And seen the soul of truth in every part,
A stedfast peace that might not be betrayed.

So once it would have been,—'tis so no more;
I have submitted to a new control:
A power is gone, which nothing can restore;   35
A deep distress hath humanised my Soul.

Not for a moment could I now behold
A smiling sea, and be what I have been:
The feeling of my loss will ne'er be old;
This, which I know, I speak with mind serene.   40

Then, Beaumont, Friend! who would have been the Friend,
If he had lived, of Him whom I deplore,
This work of thine I blame not, but commend;
This sea in anger, and that dismal shore.

O 'tis a passionate Work!—yet wise and well,   45
Well chosen is the spirit that is here;
That Hulk which labours in the deadly swell,
This rueful sky, this pageantry of fear!

And this huge Castle, standing here sublime,
I love to see the look with which it braves,   50
Cased in the unfeeling armour of old time,
The lightning, the fierce wind, and trampling waves.

Farewell, farewell the heart that lives alone,
Housed in a dream, at distance from the Kind!
Such happiness, wherever it be known,   55
Is to be pitied; for 'tis surely blind.

But welcome fortitude, and patient cheer,
And frequent sights of what is to be borne!
Such sights, or worse, as are before me here.—
Not without hope we suffer and we mourn.   60

Written after 1812 (?). *Poems* (1815)

SURPRISED by joy—impatient as the Wind
I turned to share the transport—Oh! with whom
But Thee, deep buried in the silent tomb,
That spot which no vicissitude can find?
Love, faithful love, recalled thee to my mind—   5
But how could I forget thee? Through what power,
Even for the least division of an hour,
Have I been so beguiled as to be blind
To my most grievous loss!—That thought's return
Was the worst pang that sorrow ever bore,   10
Save one, one only, when I stood forlorn,
Knowing my heart's best treasure was no more;
That neither present time, nor years unborn
Could to my sight that heavenly face restore.

FROM THE EXCURSION
1814

Book I. The Wanderer

Written 1795–8

        NINE tedious years;
From their first separation, nine long years,
She lingered in unquiet widowhood;
A Wife and Widow. Needs must it have been
A sore heart-wasting! I have heard, my Friend,   875
That in yon arbour oftentimes she sate
Alone, through half the vacant sabbath day;
And, if a dog passed by, she still would quit
The shade, and look abroad. On this old bench
For hours she sate; and evermore her eye   880
Was busy in the distance, shaping things
That made her heart beat quick. You see that path,
Now faint,—the grass has crept o'er its grey line;
There, to and fro, she paced through many a day
Of the warm summer, from a belt of hemp   885
That girt her waist, spinning the long-drawn thread
With backward steps. Yet ever as there passed
A man whose garments showed the soldier's red,
Or crippled mendicant in sailor's garb,
The little child who sate to turn the wheel   890
Ceased from his task; and she with faltering voice

Made many a fond enquiry; and when they,
Whose presence gave no comfort, were gone by,
Her heart was still more sad. And by yon gate,
That bars the traveller's road, she often stood,   895
And when a stranger horseman came, the latch
Would lift, and in his face look wistfully:
Most happy, if, from aught discovered there
Of tender feeling, she might dare repeat
The same sad question. Meanwhile her poor Hut   900
Sank to decay; for he was gone, whose hand,
At the first nipping of October frost,
Closed up each chink, and with fresh bands of straw
Chequered the green-grown thatch. And so she lived
Through the long winter, reckless and alone;   905
Until her house by frost, and thaw, and rain,
Was sapped; and while she slept, the nightly damps
Did chill her breast; and in the stormy day
Her tattered clothes were ruffled by the wind,
Even at the side of her own fire. Yet still   910
She loved this wretched spot, nor would for worlds
Have parted hence; and still that length of road,
And this rude bench, one torturing hope endeared,
Fast rooted at her heart: and here, my Friend,—
In sickness she remained; and here she died;   915
Last human tenant of these ruined walls!'

The old Man ceased: he saw that I was moved;
From that low bench, rising instinctively
I turned aside in weakness, nor had power
To thank him for the tale which he had told.   920
I stood, and leaning o'er the garden wall
Reviewed that Woman's sufferings; and it seemed
To comfort me while with a brother's love

I blessed her in the impotence of grief,
Then towards the cottage I returned; and traced   925
Fondly, though with an interest more mild,
That secret spirit of humanity
Which, 'mid the calm oblivious tendencies
Of nature, 'mid her plants, and weeds, and flowers,
And silent overgrowings, still survived.   930
The old Man, noting this, resumed, and said,
'My Friend! enough to sorrow you have given,
The purposes of wisdom ask no more:
Nor more would she have craved as due to One
Who, in her worst distress, had ofttimes felt   935
The unbounded might of prayer; and learned, with soul
Fixed on the Cross, that consolation springs,
From sources deeper far than deepest pain,
For the meek Sufferer. Why then should we read
The forms of things with an unworthy eye?   940
She sleeps in the calm earth, and peace is here.
I well remember that those very plumes,
Those weeds, and the high spear-grass on that wall,
By mist and silent rain-drops silvered o'er,
As once I passed, into my heart conveyed   945
So still an image of tranquillity,
So calm and still, and looked so beautiful
Amid the uneasy thoughts which filled my mind,
That what we feel of sorrow and despair
From ruin and from change, and all the grief   950
That passing shows of Being leave behind,
Appeared an idle dream, that could maintain,
Nowhere, dominion o'er the enlightened spirit
Whose meditative sympathies repose
Upon the breast of Faith. I turned away,   955
And walked along my road in happiness.'

He ceased. Ere long the sun declining shot
A slant and mellow radiance, which began
To fall upon us, while, beneath the trees,
We sate on that low bench: and now we felt,   960
Admonished thus, the sweet hour coming on.
A linnet warbled from those lofty elms,
A thrush sang loud, and other melodies,
At distance heard, peopled the milder air.
The old Man rose, and, with a sprightly mien   965
Of hopeful preparation, grasped his staff;
Together casting then a farewell look
Upon those silent walls, we left the shade;
And, ere the stars were visible, had reached
A village-inn,—our evening resting-place.   970

Book IV. Despondency Corrected

Written 1806?

'AND what are things eternal?—powers depart,'
The grey-haired Wanderer stedfastly replied,
Answering the question which himself had asked,
'Possessions vanish, and opinions change,
And passions hold a fluctuating seat: 70
But, by the storms of circumstance unshaken,
And subject neither to eclipse or wane,
Duty exists;—immutably survive,
For our support, the measures and the forms,
Which an abstract intelligence supplies;   75
Whose kingdom is, where time and space are not.
Of other converse which mind, soul, and heart,
Do, with united urgency, require,

What more that may not perish?—Thou, dread source,
Prime, self-existing cause and end of all   80
That in the scale of being fill their place;
Above our human region, or below,
Set and sustained;—thou, who didst wrap the cloud
Of infancy around us, that thyself,
Therein, with our simplicity awhile   85
Might'st hold, on earth, communion undisturbed;
Who from the anarchy of dreaming sleep,
Or from its death-like void, with punctual care,
And touch as gentle as the morning light,
Restor'st us, daily, to the powers of sense   90
And reason's stedfast rule—thou, thou alone
Art everlasting, and the blessed Spirits,
Which thou includest, as the sea her waves:
For adoration thou endur'st; endure
For consciousness the motions of thy will;   95
For apprehension those transcendent truths
Of the pure intellect, that stand as laws
(Submission constituting strength and power)
Even to thy Being's infinite majesty!
This universe shall pass away—a work   100
Glorious! because the shadow of thy might,
A step, or link, for intercourse with thee.
Ah! if the time must come, in which my feet
No more shall stray where meditation leads,
By flowing stream, through wood, or craggy wild,   105
Loved haunts like these; the unimprisoned Mind
May yet have scope to range among her own,
Her thoughts, her images, her high desires.
If the dear faculty of sight should fail,
Still, it may be allowed me to remember   110
What visionary powers of eye and soul

In youth were mine; when, stationed on the top
Of some huge hill—expectant, I beheld
The sun rise up, from distant climes returned
Darkness to chase, and sleep; and bring the day   115
His bounteous gift! or saw him toward the deep
Sink, with a retinue of flaming clouds
Attended; then, my spirit was entranced
With joy exalted to beatitude;
The measure of my soul was filled with bliss,   120
And holiest love; as earth, sea, air, with light,
With pomp, with glory, with magnificence!

'Those fervent raptures are for ever flown;
And, since their date, my soul hath undergone
Change manifold, for better or for worse: 125
Yet cease I not to struggle, and aspire
Heavenward; and chide the part of me that flags,
Through sinful choice; or dread necessity
On human nature from above imposed.
'Tis, by comparison, an easy task   130
Earth to despise; but, to converse with heaven—
This is not easy:—to relinquish all
We have, or hope, of happiness and joy,
And stand in freedom loosened from this world,
I deem not arduous; but must needs confess   135
That 'tis a thing impossible to frame
Conceptions equal to the soul's desires;
And the most difficult of tasks to *keep*
Heights which the soul is competent to gain.' . . .

'O blest seclusion! when the mind admits
The law of duty; and can therefore move
Through each vicissitude of loss and gain,
Linked in entire complacence with her choice;

When youth's presumptuousness is mellowed down,
And manhood's vain anxiety dismissed;   1040
When wisdom shows her seasonable fruit,
Upon the boughs of sheltering leisure hung
In sober plenty; when the spirit stoops
To drink with gratitude the crystal stream
Of unreproved enjoyment; and is pleased   1045
To muse, and be saluted by the air
Of meek repentance, wafting wall-flower scents
From out the crumbling ruins of fallen pride
And chambers of transgression, now forlorn.
O, calm contented days, and peaceful nights!   1050
Who, when such good can be obtained, would strive
To reconcile his manhood to a couch
Soft, as may seem, but, under that disguise,
Stuffed with the thorny substance of the past
For fixed annoyance; and full oft beset   1055
With floating dreams, black and disconsolate,
The vapoury phantoms of futurity?' . . .

Book IX. Discourse of the Wanderer
and an Evening Visit to the Lake

Written 1810–13

'Do not think
That good and wise ever will be allowed,   45
Though strength decay, to breathe in such estate
As shall divide them wholly from the stir
Of hopeful nature. Rightly it is said
That Man descends into the VALE of years;
Yet have I thought that we might also speak,   50

And not presumptuously, I trust, of Age,
As of a final EMINENCE; though bare
In aspect and forbidding, yet a point
On which 'tis not impossible to sit
In awful sovereignty; a place of power,   55
A throne, that may be likened unto his,
Who, in some placid day of summer, looks
Down from a mountain-top,—say one of those
High peaks, that bound the vale where now we are.
Faint, and diminished to the gazing eye,   60
Forest and field, and hill and dale appear,
With all the shapes over their surface spread:
But, while the gross and visible frame of things
Relinquishes its hold upon the sense,
Yea almost on the Mind herself, and seems   65
All unsubstantialized,—how loud the voice
Of waters, with invigorated peal
From the full river in the vale below,
Ascending! For on that superior height
Who sits, is disencumbered from the press   70
Of near obstructions, and is privileged
To breathe in solitude, above the host
Of ever-humming insects, 'mid thin air
That suits not them. The murmur of the leaves
Many and idle, visits not his ear;   75
This he is freed from, and from thousand notes
(Not less unceasing, not less vain than these,)
By which the finer passages of sense
Are occupied; and the Soul, that would incline
To listen, is prevented or deterred.   80

'And may it not be hoped, that, placed by age
In like removal, tranquil though severe,

We are not so removed for utter loss;
But for some favour, suited to our need?
What more than that the severing should confer   85
Fresh power to commune with the invisible world,
And hear the mighty stream of tendency
Uttering, for elevation of our thought,
A clear sonorous voice, inaudible
To the vast multitude; whose doom it is   90
To run the giddy round of vain delight,
Or fret and labour on the Plain below.' . . .

  'Alas! what differs more than man from man!
And whence that difference? Whence but from himself?
For see the universal Race endowed
With the same upright form!—The sun is fixed,
And the infinite magnificence of heaven   210
Fixed, within reach of every human eye;
The sleepless ocean murmurs for all ears;
The vernal field infuses fresh delight
Into all hearts. Throughout the world of sense,
Even as an object is sublime or fair   215
That object is laid open to the view
Without reserve or veil; and as a power
Is salutary, or an influence sweet,
Are each and all enabled to perceive
That power, that influence, by impartial law.   220
Gifts nobler are vouchsafed alike to all;
Reason, and, with that reason, smiles and tears;
Imagination, freedom in the will;
Conscience to guide and check; and death to be
Foretasted, immortality conceived   225
By all,—a blissful immortality,
To them whose holiness on earth shall make

The Spirit capable of heaven, assured.
Strange, then, nor less than monstrous, might be deemed
The failure, if the Almighty, to this point   230
Liberal and undistinguishing, should hide
The excellence of moral qualities
From common understanding; leaving truth
And virtue, difficult, abstruse, and dark;
Hard to be won, and only by a few;   235
Strange, should He deal herein with nice respects,
And frustrate all the rest! Believe it not:
The primal duties shine aloft—like stars;
The charities that soothe, and heal, and bless,
Are scattered at the feet of Man—like flowers.   240
The generous inclination, the just rule,
Kind wishes, and good actions, and pure thoughts—
No mystery is here! Here is no boon
For high—yet not for low; for proudly graced—
Yet not for meek of heart. The smoke ascends   245
To heaven as lightly from the cottage-hearth
As from the haughtiest palace. He, whose soul
Ponders this true equality, may walk
The fields of earth with gratitude and hope;
Yet, in that meditation, will he find   250
Motive to sadder grief, as we have found;
Lamenting ancient virtues overthrown,
And for the injustice grieving, that hath made
So wide a difference between man and man.' . . .

LATE POEMS

Composed upon an Evening of Extraordinary Splendour and Beauty

Written 1817. *Poetical Works* (1820)

I

HAD this effulgence disappeared
With flying haste, I might have sent,
Among the speechless clouds, a look
Of blank astonishment;
But 'tis endued with power to stay   5
And sanctify one closing day,
That frail Mortality may see—
What is?—ah no, but what *can* be!
Time was when field and watery cove
With modulated echoes rang,   10
While choirs of fervent Angels sang
Their vespers in the grove;
Or, crowning, star-like, each some sovereign height,
Warbled, for heaven above and earth below,
Strains suitable to both.—Such holy rite,   15
Methinks, if audibly repeated now
From hill or valley, could not move
Sublimer transport, purer love,

Than doth this silent spectacle—the gleam—
The shadow—and the peace supreme! 20

II

No sound is uttered,—but a deep
And solemn harmony pervades
The hollow vale from steep to steep,
And penetrates the glades.
Far-distant images draw nigh, 25
Called forth by wondrous potency
Of beamy radiance, that imbues
Whate'er it strikes with gem-like hues!
In vision exquisitely clear,
Herds range along the mountain side; 30
And glistening antlers are descried;
And gilded flocks appear.
This is the tranquil hour, purpureal Eve!
But long as god-like wish, or hope divine,
Informs my spirit, ne'er can I believe 35
That this magnificence is wholly thine!
—From worlds not quickened by the sun
A portion of the gift is won;
An intermingling of Heaven's pomp is spread
On grounds which British shepherds tread! 40

III

And, if there be whom broken ties
Afflict, or injuries assail,
Yon hazy ridges to their eyes
Present a glorious scale,
Climbing suffused with sunny air, 45
To stop—no record hath told where!

And tempting Fancy to ascend,
And with immortal Spirits blend!
—Wings at my shoulders seem to play;
But, rooted here, I stand and gaze   50
On those bright steps that heavenward raise
Their practicable way.
Come forth, ye drooping old men, look abroad,
And see to what fair countries ye are bound!
And if some traveller, weary of his road,   55
Hath slept since noon-tide on the grassy ground,
Ye Genii! to his covert speed;
And wake him with such gentle heed
As may attune his soul to meet the dower
Bestowed on this transcendent hour!   60

IV

Such hues from their celestial Urn
Were wont to stream before mine eye,
Where'er it wandered in the morn
Of blissful infancy.
This glimpse of glory, why renewed?   65
Nay, rather speak with gratitude;
For, if a vestige of those gleams
Survived, 'twas only in my dreams.
Dread Power! whom peace and calmness serve
No less than Nature's threatening voice,   70
If aught unworthy be my choice,
From THEE if I would swerve;
Oh, let Thy grace remind me of the light
Full early lost, and fruitlessly deplored;
Which, at this moment, on my waking sight   75
Appears to shine, by miracle restored;

My soul, though yet confined to earth,
Rejoices in a second birth!
—'Tis past, the visionary splendour fades;
And night approaches with her shades.   80

Note.—The multiplication of mountain-ridges, described at the commence-
ment of the third Stanza of this Ode as a kind of Jacob's Ladder, leading to
Heaven, is produced either by watery vapours, or sunny haze;—in the present
instance by the latter cause. Allusions to the Ode entitled 'Intimations of Immortality' pervade the last Stanza of the foregoing Poem.

After-Thought

Written 1820. *The River Duddon, A Series of Sonnets* (1820)

I THOUGHT of Thee, my partner and my guide,
As being past away.—Vain sympathies!
For, backward, Duddon! as I cast my eyes,
I see what was, and is, and will abide;
Still glides the Stream, and shall for ever glide;   5
The Form remains, the Function never dies;
While we, the brave, the mighty, and the wise,
We Men, who in our morn of youth defied
The elements, must vanish;—be it so!
Enough, if something from our hands have power   10
To live, and act, and serve the future hour;
And if, as toward the silent tomb we go,
Through love, through hope, and faith's transcendent dower,
We feel that we are greater than we know.

Inside of King's College Chapel, Cambridge

Written 1820. *Ecclesiastical Sketches* (1822)

TAX not the royal Saint with vain expense,
With ill-matched aims the Architect who planned—
Albeit labouring for a scanty band
Of white-robed Scholars only—this immense
And glorious Work of fine intelligence!   5
Give all thou canst; high Heaven rejects the lore
Of nicely-calculated less or more;
So deemed the man who fashioned for the sense
These lofty pillars, spread that branching roof
Self-poised, and scooped into ten thousand cells,   10
Where light and shade repose, where music dwells
Lingering—and wandering on as loth to die;
Like thoughts whose very sweetness yieldeth proof
That they were born for immortality.

Mutability

Written 1821. *Ecclesiastical Sketches* (1822)

FROM low to high doth dissolution climb,
And sink from high to low, along a scale
Of awful notes, whose concord shall not fail;
A musical but melancholy chime,
Which they can hear who meddle not with crime,   5
Nor avarice, nor over-anxious care.
Truth fails not; but her outward forms that bear
The longest date do melt like frosty rime,

That in the morning whitened hill and plain
And is no more; drop like the tower sublime 10
Of yesterday, which royally did wear
His crown of weeds, but could not even sustain
Some casual shout that broke the silent air,
Or the unimaginable touch of Time.

Written after May 1825. *Poetical Works* (1827)

WHILE Anna's peers and early playmates tread,
In freedom, mountain-turf and river's marge;
Or float with music in the festal barge;
Rein the proud steed, or through the dance are led;
Her doom it is to press a weary bed— 5
Till oft her guardian Angel, to some charge
More urgent called, will stretch his wings at large,
And friends too rarely prop the languid head.
Yet, helped by Genius—untired comforter,
The presence even of a stuffed Owl for her 10
Can cheat the time; sending her fancy out
To ivied castles and to moonlight skies,
Though he can neither stir a plume, nor shout;
Nor veil, with restless film, his staring eyes.

Airey-Force Valley

Written 1835. *Poetical Works* (1842)

————NOT a breath of air
Ruffles the bosom of this leafy glen.
From the brook's margin, wide around, the trees
Are steadfast as the rocks; the brook itself,
Old as the hills that feed it from afar, 5
Doth rather deepen than disturb the calm

Where all things else are still and motionless.
And yet, even now, a little breeze, perchance
Escaped from boisterous winds that rage without,
Has entered, by the sturdy oaks unfelt,   10
But to its gentle touch how sensitive
Is the light ash! that, pendent from the brow
Of yon dim cave, in seeming silence makes
A soft eye-music of slow-waving boughs,
Powerful almost as vocal harmony   15
To stay the wanderer's steps and soothe his thoughts.

Extempore Effusion upon the Death of James Hogg

Written 1835. *Poetical Works* (1837)

WHEN first, descending from the moorlands,
I saw the Stream of Yarrow glide
Along a bare and open valley,
The Ettrick Shepherd was my guide.

When last along its banks I wandered,   5
Through groves that had begun to shed
Their golden leaves upon the pathways,
My steps the Border-minstrel led.

The mighty Minstrel breathes no longer,
'Mid mouldering ruins low he lies;   10
And death upon the braes of Yarrow,
Has closed the Shepherd-poet's eyes:

Nor has the rolling year twice measured,
From sign to sign, its stedfast course,
Since every mortal power of Coleridge   15
Was frozen at its marvellous source;

The rapt One, of the godlike forehead,
The heaven-eyed creature sleeps in earth:
And Lamb, the frolic and the gentle,
Has vanished from his lonely hearth.   20

Like clouds that rake the mountain-summits,
Or waves that own no curbing hand,
How fast has brother followed brother,
From sunshine to the sunless land!

Yet I, whose lids from infant slumber   25
Were earlier raised, remain to hear
A timid voice, that asks in whispers,
'Who next will drop and disappear?'

Our haughty life is crowned with darkness,
Like London with its own black wreath,   30
On which with thee, O Crabbe! forth-looking,
I gazed from Hampstead's breezy heath.

As if but yesterday departed,
Thou too art gone before; but why,
O'er ripe fruit, seasonably gathered,   35
Should frail survivors heave a sigh?

Mourn rather for that holy Spirit,
Sweet as the spring, as ocean deep;
For Her who, ere her summer faded,
Has sunk into a breathless sleep.   40

No more of old romantic sorrows,
For slaughtered Youth or love-lorn Maid!
With sharper grief is Yarrow smitten,
And Ettrick mourns with her their Poet dead.

FROM THE PREFACE TO
LYRICAL BALLADS
(1800)

THE principal object, then, proposed in these Poems was to choose incidents and situations from common life, and to relate or describe them, throughout, as far as was possible in a selection of language really used by men, and, at the same time, to throw over them a certain colouring of imagination, whereby ordinary things should be presented to the mind in an unusual aspect; and, further, and above all, to make these incidents and situations interesting by tracing in them, truly though not ostentatiously, the primary laws of our nature: chiefly, as far as regards the manner in which we associate ideas in a state of excitement. Humble and rustic life was generally chosen, because, in that condition, the essential passions of the heart find a better soil in which they can attain their maturity, are less under restraint, and speak a plainer and more emphatic language; because in that condition of life our elementary feelings coexist in a state of greater simplicity, and consequently, may be more accurately contemplated, and more forcibly communicated; because the manners of rural life germinate from those elementary feelings, and, from the necessary character of rural occupations, are more easily comprehended, and are more durable; and, lastly, because in that condition the passions of men are incorporated with the beautiful and permanent forms of nature. The language, too, of these men has been adopted (purified indeed from what appear to be its real defects, from all lasting and rational causes of dislike or disgust) because such men hourly communicate with the best objects from which the best part of language is originally derived; and because, from their rank in society and the sameness and narrow circle of their intercourse, being less under the influence of social vanity, they convey their feelings and notions in simple and unelaborated expressions. Accordingly, such a language, arising out of repeated experience and regular feelings, is a more permanent, and a far more philosophical language, than that which is frequently substituted for it by Poets, who think that they are conferring honour upon themselves and their art, in proportion as they separate themselves from the sympathies of men, and indulge in arbitrary and capricious habits of expression, in order to furnish food for fickle tastes, and fickle appetites, of their own creation.

I cannot, however, be insensible to the present outcry against the triviality and meanness, both of thought and language, which some of my contemporaries have occasionally introduced into their metrical compositions; and I acknowledge that this defect, where it exists, is more dishonourable to the Writer's own character than false refinement or arbitrary innovation, though I should contend at the same time, that it is far less pernicious in the sum of its consequences. From such verses the Poems in these volumes will be found distinguished at least by one mark of difference, that each of them has a worthy *purpose*. Not that I always began to write with a distinct purpose formally conceived; but habits of meditation have, I trust, so prompted and regulated my feelings, that my descriptions of such objects as strongly excite those feelings, will be found to carry along with them a *purpose*. If this opinion be erroneous, I can have little right to the name of a Poet. For all good poetry is the spontaneous overflow of powerful feelings: and though this be true, Poems to which any value can be attached were never produced on any variety of subjects but by a man who, being possessed of more than usual organic sensibility, had also thought long and deeply. For our continued influxes of feeling are modified and directed by our thoughts, which are indeed the representatives of all our past feelings; and, as by contemplating the relation of these general representatives to each other, we discover what is really important to men, so, by the repetition and continuance of this act, our feelings will be connected with important subjects, till at length, if we be originally possessed of much sensibility, such habits of mind will be produced, that, by obeying blindly and mechanically the impulses of those habits, we shall describe objects, and utter sentiments, of such a nature, and in such connection with each other, that the understanding of the Reader must necessarily be in some degree enlightened, and his affections strengthened and purified. . . .

Taking up the subject, then, upon general grounds, let me ask, what is meant by the word Poet? What is a Poet? To whom does he address himself? And what language is to be expected from him?—He is a man speaking to men: a man, it is true, endowed with more lively sensibility, more enthusiasm and tenderness, who has a greater knowledge of human nature, and a more comprehensive soul, than are supposed to be common among mankind; a man pleased with his own passions and volitions, and who rejoices more than other men in the spirit of life that is in him; delighting to contemplate similar volitions and passions as manifested in the goings-on of the Universe, and habitually impelled to create them where he does not find them. To these qualities he has added a disposition to be affected more than other men by absent things as if they were present; an ability of conjuring up in himself passions, which are indeed far from being the same as those produced by real events, yet (especially in those parts of the general sympathy which are pleasing and delightful) do more nearly resemble the passions produced by real events, than anything which, from the motions of their own minds merely, other men are accustomed to feel in themselves:—whence, and from practice, he has acquired a greater readiness and power in expressing what he thinks and feels, and especially those thoughts and feelings which, by his own choice, or from the structure of his own mind, arise in him without immediate external excitement. . . .

I have said that poetry is the spontaneous overflow of powerful feelings: it takes its origin from emotion recollected in tranquillity: the emotion is contemplated till, by a species of reaction, the tranquillity gradually disappears, and an emotion, kindred to that which was before the subject of contemplation, is gradually produced, and does itself actually exist in the mind. In this mood successful composition generally begins, and in a mood similar to this it is carried on. . . .

APPENDIX

Extracts from Dorothy Wordsworth's *Journal*

1. [See 'Resolution and Independence', p. 145.]

October 3rd, Friday [*1800*]. Very rainy all the morning. Little Sally learning to mark. Wm. walked to Ambleside after dinner, I went with him part of the way. He talked much about the object of his Essay for the second volume of 'L.B.' I returned expecting the Simpsons—they did not come. I should have met Wm. but my teeth ached and it was showery and late—he returned after 10. Amos Cottle's death in the *Morning Post*. Wrote to S. Lowthian.

N.B. When Wm. and I returned from accompanying Jones, we met an old man almost double. He had on a coat, thrown over his shoulders, above his waistcoat and coat. Under this he carried a bundle, and had an apron on and a night-cap. His face was interesting. He had dark eyes and a long nose. John, who afterwards met him at Wythburn, took him for a Jew. He was of Scotch parents, but had been born in the army. He had had a wife, and 'a good woman, and it pleased God to bless us with ten children'. All these were dead but one, of whom he had not heard for many years, a sailor. His trade was to gather leeches, but now leeches are scarce, and he had not strength for it. He lived by begging, and was making his way to Carlisle, where he should buy a few godly books to sell. He said leeches were very scarce, partly owing to this dry season, but many years they have been scarce—he supposed it owing to their being much sought after, that they did not breed fast, and were of slow growth. Leeches were formerly 2s. 6d. [per] 100; they are now 30s. He had been hurt in driving a cart, his leg broke, his body driven over, his skull fractured. He felt no pain till he recovered from his first insensibility. It was then late in the evening, when the light was just going away.

2. [See 'I wandered lonely as a cloud', p. 153.]

[*April*] *15th. Thursday* [*1802*]. It was a threatening, misty morning, but mild. We set off after dinner from Eusemere. Mrs. Clarkson went a short way with us, but turned back. The wind was furious, and we thought we must have returned. We first rested in the large Boat-house, then under a furze bush opposite Mr. Clarkson's. Saw the plough going in the field. The wind seized our breath. The Lake was rough. There was a Boat by itself floating in the middle of the Bay below Water Millock. We rested again in the Water Millock Lane. The hawthorns are black and green, the birches here and there greenish, but there is yet more of purple to be seen on the twigs. We got over into a field to avoid some cows—people working. A few primroses by the roadside—woodsorrel flower, the anemone, scentless violets, strawberries, and that starry, yellow flower which Mrs. C. calls pile wort. When we were in the woods beyond Gowbarrow park we saw a few daffodils close to the water-side. We fancied that the lake had floated the seeds ashore, and that the little colony had so sprung up. But as we went along there were more and yet more; and at last, under the boughs of the trees, we saw that there was a long belt of them along the shore, about the breadth of a country turnpike road. I never saw daffodils so beautiful. They grew among the mossy stones about and about them; some rested their heads upon these stones as on a pillow for weariness; and the rest tossed and reeled and danced, and seemed as if they verily laughed with the wind, that blew upon them over the lake; they looked so gay, ever glancing, ever changing. This wind blew directly over the lake to them. There was here and there a little knot, and a few stragglers a few yards higher up; but they were so few as not to disturb the simplicity, unity, and life of that one busy highway. We rested again and again. The bays were stormy, and we heard the waves at different distances, and in the middle of the water, like the sea. Rain came in—we were wet when we reached Luff's, but we called in. Luckily all was chearless and gloomy, so we faced the storm—we *must* have been wet if we had waited—put on dry clothes at Dobson's. I was very kindly treated by a young woman, the Landlady looked sour, but it is her way. She gave us a goodish supper, excellent ham and potatoes. We paid 7/- when we came away. William was sitting by a bright fire when I came downstairs. He soon made his way to the library, piled up in a corner of the window. He brought out a volume of Enfield's *Speaker*, another miscellany, and an odd volume of Congreve's plays. We had a glass of warm rum and water. We enjoyed ourselves, and wished for Mary. It rained and blew when we went to bed. N.B. Deer in Gowbarrow park like skeletons.

NOTES TO THE POEMS

PAGE 39. 'PROSPECTUS.' These lines were published at the end of the preface to *The Excursion* 'as a kind of *Prospectus* of the design and scope of the whole Poem'. They also provide a 'prospectus' of his entire work in that they draw attention to the theme (l. 1) of this essentially solitary observer (l. 2); the philosophical character of his work (ll. 14–17), and its 'joy' (l. 18); they point to 'the Mind of Man' as the principal topic (ll. 40–41), but more particularly to the Mind 'wedded to this goodly universe' (l. 53), and the 'creation' (l. 69) which thence ensues. They were designed to conclude the first book of *The Recluse*.

18. *commonalty*: The general body of the community. Wordsworth held no esoteric views about poetry. He looked upon himself as a man speaking to men, awakening their minds from 'the lethargy of custom'.

25. *Urania*: The heavenly Muse, invoked by Milton in *Paradise Lost*, VII (from which Wordsworth quotes at l. 23). She 'with eternal Wisdom did'st converse'.

95. *the Mind and Man contemplating*: i.e. himself, the theme of *The Prelude*.

PAGE 43. THE PRELUDE. The poem opens with a long preamble describing the poet's walk from Bristol to Racedown in 1795, when he dedicated himself to 'some work of glory'. The difficulties and delays that baffled his efforts are recalled in a passage probably written in 1803, and the autobiographical narrative then begins, at Cockermouth, with l. 271.

I. 302. The ministry of beauty and of fear in his upbringing is developed over the next 250 lines.

304. *that beloved Vale*: Hawkshead in Esthwaite, north Lancashire, west of Windermere, where he spent his school-days, 1779–87.

340–55. This meditative passage serves to separate the first two incidents, in the first of which Nature had employed 'fearless visitings' (l. 352) and in the second 'soft alarm' (l. 353), from the 'severer interventions' (l. 355) of the third.

342–4. The reconciling of discordant elements is grandly illustrated at VI. 624–40 (p. 64).

349. *The calm existence*: such 'settled quietness' was already envied in

'Animal Tranquillity and Decay' (p. 83). See also 'Ode to Duty', l. 40 (p. 188), and pp. 197–8.

357–400. In the 1805 version Wordsworth mentioned that this famous episode took place 'by the shores of Patterdale'. Characteristically (cf. p. 221) he removed the unduly particular reference; but thereby he confused readers who vainly tried to locate a scene, well suited to the rocky shore and mountainous environs of Ullswater, in the gently sloping country round Esthwaite.

430. *a time of rapture*: so defined also in 'Tintern Abbey', l. 85.

432. *an untired horse*: the simile is appropriate to what he called the 'glad animal movements' of his 'boyish days'. See 'Tintern Abbey', ll. 67, 73, 74.

425–52. The passage was significantly heightened in revision. Cf. the following readings from the 1805 text:

> 437. The Pack loud bellowing . . .
> 440. Meanwhile, the precipices . . .
> 450. To cut across the image of a star
>   That gleam'd upon the ice: and oftentimes

460. *diurnal round*: for thought and phrasing, cf. 'A slumber did my spirit seal', l. 7 (p. 136).

517. *not, as in the world*: the negative simile, so reminiscent of *Paradise Lost*, prepares for the mock-heroic treatment of the card-games, as in Pope's *Rape of the Lock*, which is intentionally recalled at l. 522: 'Gain'd but one Trump, and one *Plebeian* Card' (iii. 54).

527. *ironic*: because so much the reverse of bright. The grubbiness of the much-used pack is recalled throughout the next eight lines.

535–43. A characteristic 'crescendo' to the end of the paragraph, and a calculated contrast of the 'beautiful' with the 'sublime' (l. 546) according to the best principles of Burkeian aesthetics.

555–8. He had already declared his theme to be how the Mind is fitted to the World (p. 41, l. 65).

II. 103. *that large abbey*: Furness Abbey, 21 miles distant from Hawkshead.

137. The whole passage is recalled and this last line used in triumphant conclusion to *The Prelude*, X, on hearing the news of Robespierre's death.

361–2. He was always conscious of the danger of taking things for granted, and had assumed for his share in *Lyrical Ballads* (according to Coleridge) that of 'awakening the mind's attention from the lethargy of custom, and directing it to the loveliness and the wonders of the world before us'. Compare 'Ode', ll. 127-9 (p. 184), 'Tintern Abbey', ll. 130-4 (p. 114).

362-74. The quality of the youthful poet's 'creative sensibility' is more emphatically called in question in 'Elegiac Stanzas' (p. 189), though even there (as here, ll. 366-8) it is true to his experience at that age. Here perhaps he comes closest to Coleridge's view ('Lines Written . . . at Elbingerode', ll. 17, 18):

> That outward forms, the loftiest, still receive
> Their finer influence from the Life within.

384-6. The associative principle extends beyond the mere operation of the Fancy ('chance collisions and quaint accidents', *The Prelude*, I. 589) to that of the Imagination, which declares the true kinship of all created things. With ll. 389-418, compare *The Prelude*, VI. 624-40 (p. 64), VIII. 365-432 (pp. 67).

432 ff. Written in response to Coleridge's request (1799) for an address 'to those, who, in consequence of the complete failure of the French Revolution, have thrown up all hopes of the amelioration of mankind, and are sinking into an almost epicurean selfishness, disguising the same under the soft titles of domestic attachment [l. 438] and contempt for visionary *philosophes*' [ll. 439-40].

III. 1-63. Written in a humbler, more ironic vein (note ll. 25-28, 38-42), after the manner of Cowper's *Task*, except for the splendid ll. 62-63, added when he was over sixty years old.

46-48. Wordsworth's rooms at St. John's College were removed in a late nineteenth-century alteration.

IV. 309-38. An early instance of revelation in mystical experience. Like similar instances, e.g. *The Prelude*, VI. 617 (p. 64), it occurred after a period of great physical activity, trivial in kind (see IV. 374-8).

321. *kindling*: a recollection of Thomson's description of dawn in *Summer* (l. 83), where the azure is said to be 'kindling'.

328. *grain-tinctured*: a recollection of Milton's 'sky-tinctur'd grain' (*Paradise Lost*, v. 285); cochineal-coloured.

371-469. An illustration of 'how benign is Solitude',

> When from our better selves we have too long
> Been parted by the hurrying world. (IV. 354-7)

379. He was walking back to Hawkshead through Sawrey from Windermere Ferry.

432. *To travel without pain*: cf. 'Animal Tranquillity and Decay', l. 6

(p. 83). The 'quiet, uncomplaining voice' (l. 419) and the absence of feeling (l. 445) also recall this poem.

VI. 570. His route has been traced by Max Wildi in an illustrated article, 'Wordsworth and the Simplon Pass', *English Studies*, xl (1959), 224–32.

592–614. This great testimony to the power of the Imagination prepares for the illustration that follows of the Imagination in action, particularly the recognition, in ll. 624 ff., that so many seemingly discordant phenomena bore to each other the same intimate relationship as do 'features of the same face'.

599–602. What characterizes the moment of insight is described in similar terms in 'Tintern Abbey', ll. 43–49 (p. 111).

VIII. 215–22. A passage overlooked by those who claim that Wordsworth's doctrines could not have been developed except in temperate regions, and an impressive testimony to the discipline of fear (*The Prelude*, I. 302, 413; pp. 43, 46).

253. *A freeman*: like Michael. The whole passage should be read in connexion with that poem.

275. *Chartreuse*: he had noted in *Descriptive Sketches* (1793) 'The Cross, by angels planted on the aerial rock', and had remarked in a footnote that these 'spiry rocks of the Chartreuse . . . have every appearance of being inaccessible'.

285, 287. *Corin . . . Phyllis*: names familiar in Elizabethan pastoral.

373 ff. Wordsworth emphasizes the playfulness and irresponsibility of the associations made by the Fancy:

> yet not vain
> Nor profitless, if haply they impressed
> Collateral objects and appearances,
> Albeit lifeless then, and doomed to sleep
> Until maturer seasons called them forth
> To impregnate and elevate the mind.

The Prelude, I. 591–6; and compare II. 384–6 (p. 53), and note.

XI. 266–305. Books IX, X, and XI relate his experiences during a visit to France (November 1791 to January 1793) in the throes of revolution: his political instruction at the hands of Beaupuy, his sympathy with the republican cause, the effect upon him of the September massacres, his subsequent distress at British intervention and at the Reign of Terror. The turmoil in his mind and the spiritual crisis is described in this extract.

XII. 221–2. An illustration of his claim to have sung not only of the Mind being fitted to the external world, but also 'how exquisitely . . . The external World is fitted to the Mind' (p. 41).

269–79. As impressive a testimony as the 'Ode' itself (ll. 150–7, pp. 184–5) to the source, in childhood, of his poetic strength.

PAGE 76. THE OLD CUMBERLAND BEGGAR. 'Observed, and with great benefit to my own heart, when I was a child: written at Racedown and Alfoxden. . . . The political economists were about that time beginning their war upon mendicity in all its forms, and by implication, if not directly, on Almsgiving also.'

34. *wheel*: spinning-wheel.

61. *cottage curs*: a recollection of a phrase in Beattie's *Minstrel*, 1771, st. 39: 'the cottage curs at early pilgrim bark'.

89. *binds*: the verb and the associated thought recur in 'My heart leaps up', l. 9 (p. 179).

110–16: for the thought in this passage, compare 'Lines written in Early Spring', ll. 5–8 (p. 99), and 'The Tables Turned' (p. 98).

153. Quoted by Wordsworth in a letter to Crabb Robinson, 1835: 'If my writings are to last it will, I myself believe, be mainly owing to this characteristic. They will please for the single cause, "that we have all of us one human heart!" '

179. 'House of Industry', or workhouse, was the name given to an institution set up in a parish to provide work for unemployed poor.

PAGE 83. ANIMAL TRANQUILLITY AND DECAY. An 'overflowing' from the previous poem; it explores the old man's inner state.

13. This yearning for calmness is characteristic. Compare *The Prelude*, I. 349–50 (p. 44).

14. In 1798 the poem ended with six lines subsequently omitted because, presumably, they are unduly particular. Compare *The Prelude*, I. 357–400 n. (p. 218):

> I asked him whither he was bound, and what
> The object of his journey; he replied
> 'Sir! I am going many miles to take
> A last leave of my son, a mariner,
> Who from a sea-fight has been brought to Falmouth,
> And there is dying in an hospital.——'

PAGE 84. GOODY BLAKE AND HARRY GILL. In his 'Advertisement' to *Lyrical Ballads*, 1798, Wordsworth states that the poem 'is founded on a well-authenticated fact which happened in Warwickshire'. He had read the story in Erasmus Darwin's *Zoonomia, or the Laws of Organic Life*, 1794–6. In his 'Preface', 1800, he explained that he 'wished to draw attention to the truth that the power of the human imagination is sufficient to produce such changes even in our physical nature as might almost appear miraculous'.

17. *drover*: a dealer in cattle.

29–32. A notable improvement of 1820 and subsequent revisions upon the original version, which ran:

> This woman dwelt in Dorsetshire,
> Her hut was on a cold hill-side,
> And in that country coals are dear,
> For they come far by wind and tide.

39. *canty*: cheerful: a north-country term.

PAGE 88. SIMON LEE. Wordsworth reported (in spite of l. 1) that 'this old man had been huntsman to the Squires of Alfoxden'. None of his shorter poems was subjected to so much revision, the object apparently being to broaden the contrast between Simon Lee's youth and age.

24. 'The expression . . . was word for word from his lips.' For other instances of his adopting 'the very language of men' (as he proposed in his preface to *Lyrical Ballads*, 1800), see 'The Sailor's Mother' (p. 142); 'Stepping Westward', l. 1 (p. 166).

25. *But, oh the heavy change!*: the poetical context seems radically unsuited to this borrowing from *Lycidas*, l. 37.

60. A doubtful improvement of 1815 upon the original reading 'His poor old ancles swell'.

PAGE 91. ANECDOTE FOR FATHERS. In 1798 the poem carried the subtitle 'Shewing how the art of lying may be taught'. The quotation from Eusebius is a translation of the Delphic oracle's rebuke to those who tried to extort an answer by force: 'Don't use violence, for I shall tell lies, if you force me.' The incident was suggested at Alfoxden, Somerset, where the Wordsworths stayed for several months in 1797–8. 'The Boy was a son of my friend Basil Montagu, who had been two or three years under our care. The name of Kilve is from a village on the Bristol Channel, about a mile from Alfoxden; and the name of Liswyn Farm was taken from a beautiful spot on the Wye.' See p. 11.

PAGE 94. WE ARE SEVEN. Also written at Alfoxden. Wordsworth recorded that he 'composed the last stanza first, having begun with the last line', and that Coleridge 'threw off' the first stanza as a preface. The poem was intended to show 'the perplexity and obscurity which in childhood attend our notion of death, or rather our utter inability to admit that notion'. The little girl possesses an 'intimation of immortality'.

PAGE 96. EXPOSTULATION AND REPLY.   These lines 'and those that follow, arose out of conversation with a friend [Hazlitt] who was somewhat unreasonably attached to modern books of moral philosophy'. But by 'Matthew' (l. 15) Wordsworth seems to have meant his old schoolmaster at Hawkshead (near Esthwaite, l. 13), Edward Taylor.

PAGE 99. LINES WRITTEN IN EARLY SPRING.

1. *notes*: the rhyme with 'thoughts' is still quite acceptable to Cumberland ears.

5, 6. Another instance of the 'primal sympathy' of *The Prelude*, I. 551–8 (p. 50) and the 'Immortality' Ode, ll. 182–3 (p. 185).

11–20. For this way of thinking, compare 'Ode to Duty', ll. 53–56 (p. 188).

21–22. This version was not reached until 1837. From 1798 the lines read, clumsily:

> If I these thoughts may not prevent,
> If such be of my creed the plan.

PAGE 100. TO MY SISTER.   The poem was 'composed in front of Alfoxden House. My little boy-messenger . . . was the son of Basil Montagu', the 'Edward' of 'Anecdote for Fathers'.

PAGE 102. THE LAST OF THE FLOCK. See p. 11.

PAGE 106. HER EYES ARE WILD. This poem was first entitled 'The Mad Mother'. The poem was designed 'to illustrate the manner in which our feelings and ideas are associated in a state of excitement . . . [more particularly] by tracing the maternal passion through many of its more subtle windings'. Wordsworth seems to have been affected by two poems in that favourite collection, Percy's *Reliques*: it contains a section of 'Mad Songs', one of them, 'The Frantic Lady', beginning:

> I burn, my brain consumes to ashes!
> Each eye-ball too like lightning flashes!
> Within my breast there glows a solid fire,
> Which in a thousand ages can't expire;

'Lady Anne Bothwell's Lament' (not one of the 'Mad Songs') is a monologue spoken by a deserted woman to the baby at her breast, who both reminds her of his father's falsehood, and whose 'winsome smiles maun eise my paine'.

PAGE 110. LINES COMPOSED A FEW MILES ABOVE TINTERN ABBEY.

'I began it upon leaving Tintern after crossing the Wye, and concluded it just as I was entering Bristol in the evening, after a ramble of 4 or 5 days, with my sister. Not a line of it was altered, and not any part of it written down till I reached Bristol. It was published almost immediately after', taking the place in *Lyrical Ballads* that might have been more suitably occupied by *Peter Bell*. But though not a ballad nor even strictly lyrical, 'it was written (said Wordsworth) with a hope that in the transitions, and the impassioned music of the versification, would be found the principal requisites of' an ode.

2. He visited Tintern in 1793, after leaving the Isle of Wight on his way to North Wales.

22–30. For the thought compare 'I wandered lonely as a cloud', ll. 19–24 (p. 154).

30–35. For the spontaneity of the response, the absence of the will and the reason, compare 'The Old Cumberland Beggar', ll. 99–105 (p. 79), 'The Tables Turned', ll. 19–32 (p. 98).

35–49. For accounts of similar mystical experiences, when 'laid asleep in body', see *The Prelude*, IV. 309–38 (p. 58), VI. 592–640 (p. 63).

66. *changed*: i.e. from what he was at the age of 23.

80, 83. *appetite . . . Unborrowed from the eye*: for other expressions of this craving and of the eye's despotic power, compare *The Prelude*, XII. 127–47:

> I speak in recollection of a time
> When the bodily eye, in every stage of life
> The most despotic of our senses, gained
> Such strength in *me* as often held my mind
> In absolute dominion. . . . Enough that my delights
> (Such as they were) were sought insatiably.
> Vivid the transport, vivid though not profound.

100–2. This recognition of unity in diversity is even more memorably expressed in *The Prelude*, VI. 624–40 (p. 64).

106. The line in Young's *Night-Thoughts* (1744), which Wordsworth could not quite recall, reads (vi. 424): 'And half-create the wondrous world they see.'

PAGE 116. THERE WAS A BOY. Incorporated in *The Prelude*, V. 364–97. The poem illustrates one of the psychological processes by which 'even in what seem our most unfruitful hours . . . a wiser spirit is at work for us', storing the mind with tranquillizing images such as may be recalled, as he describes in 'I wandered lonely as a cloud' (p. 154) and the Tintern Abbey 'Lines' (p. 111). An early draft shows that the passage was autobiographical.

PAGE 117. NUTTING. Intended as part of *The Prelude*, but omitted because not needed.

11. *my frugal Dame*: Anne Tyson, with whom he lived when he attended Hawkshead School. See p. 51, l. 87.

PAGE 119. MICHAEL. Wordsworth said he had 'attempted to give a picture of a man, of strong mind and lively sensibility, agitated by two of the most powerful affections of the human heart; the parental affection, and the love of property, *landed* property, including the feelings of inheritance, home, and personal and family independence'. It showed 'the domestic affections as I know they exist amongst . . . small independent proprietors of land'. Luke's character was taken from a member of a family who had once owned Wordsworth's cottage.

2. *Green-head ghyll*: at the north-east of the vale of Grasmere.

11. *kites*: formerly a common bird of prey in Britain, but now exceptionally rare.

24. *Whom I . . . loved*: compare *The Prelude*, VIII. 223–93 (p. 65).

29–33. Compare 'Tintern Abbey', ll. 88–91 (p. 113), and *The Prelude*, VIII. 275–9 (p. 66).

58–60. Compare *The Prelude*, VIII. 264–6 (p. 66).

258. *Richard Bateman*: he rebuilt Ings Chapel, between Kendal and Windermere, in 1743.

324. *Sheep-fold*: Wordsworth explained in a note that a sheep-fold is 'an unroofed building of stone walls, with different divisions. It is generally placed by the side of a brook, for the convenience of washing the sheep; but it is also useful as a shelter', and as a place where they can be driven for singling out.

PAGE 134. THE REVERIE OF POOR SUSAN. In the edition of 1815 Wordsworth placed this poem to follow 'I wandered lonely as a cloud', with which it has obvious affinities. He also removed the final verse, which read:

> Poor Outcast! return—to receive thee once more
> The house of thy Father will open its door,
> And thou once again, in thy plain russet gown,
> May'st hear the thrush sing from a tree of its own.

Perhaps he accepted the force of Lamb's protest, that 'it threw a kind of dubiety upon Susan's moral conduct'. Lothbury and Cheapside are streets in the City of London.

PAGE 135. 'THREE YEARS SHE GREW.' This and the three following poems form a group of studies in solitude and environment. The first three were written at Goslar in Germany, the fourth on his return. Speculation about the identity of Lucy has been fruitless; her name is commonly met in eighteenth-century pastoral ballads.

PAGE 140. THE SPARROW'S NEST. A striking testimony to the influence of Dorothy Wordsworth, whose Christian name appears in l. 9 in the manuscript. 'Emmeline' seems to have been taken from 'The Child of Elle', a ballad largely composed by Percy for his *Reliques of Ancient English Poetry*.

PAGE 140. 'SHE WAS A PHANTOM OF DELIGHT.' A tribute to Mrs. Wordsworth.

22. *machine*: the human body regarded as a combination of several parts. Wordsworth may have recalled a passage from Bartram's *Travels*: 'at the return of morning, by the powerful influence of light, the *pulse* of nature becomes more active, and the universal vibration of life insensibly and irresistibly moves the wondrous *machine*'.

PAGE 141. THE SAILOR'S MOTHER. Wordsworth records that he met the woman on the high road between Grasmere and Ambleside: 'Her appearance was exactly as here described, and such was her account, nearly to the letter.' The last three stanzas 'furnish the only instance . . . in all Mr. Wordsworth's writings, of an *actual* adoption, or true imitation, of the *real* and *very* language of *low and rustic* life, freed from provincialisms' (Coleridge).

22–23. The original version of these lines reads:
> And I have been as far as Hull to see
> What clothes he might have left, or other property.

The revision, made in 1827, characteristically removed topographical and other extraneous detail (cf. p. 45, l. 357, p. 83, l. 14, with notes on pp. 218, 221), while avoiding bathos.

PAGE 143. BEGGARS. This poem, which was written within a few days of 'The Sailor's Mother', depended not on a personal encounter, but on a story recorded by Dorothy Wordsworth in her Journal and read to William: 'An unlucky thing it was, for he could not escape from those very words, and so he could not write the poem.' Nevertheless he finished it the next morning. Wordsworth told Crabb Robinson that the poem was written 'to exhibit the power of physical beauty and health and vigour in childhood even in a state of moral depravity'; on another occasion he said he had 'aimed at giving . . . elegance and dignity to this poem'.

21–22. Except for the colour, the detail is from the Journal.

24. The first five words are taken from the Journal.

25–26. The detail and phrasing come from the Journal.

31–36. The stanza was added in 1827, perhaps to help in 'pointing the moral', perhaps to give more 'elegance and dignity'.

PAGE 145. RESOLUTION AND INDEPENDENCE. The incident on which the poem is based was recorded in Dorothy Wordsworth's Journal, and is reprinted on p. 214. The theme of the poem required the time of day and season of the year to be altered, and the poet's companion to be removed. The setting is also changed, from a frequented to a lonely spot. Wordsworth recorded that he 'was in the state of feeling described in the beginning of the poem, while crossing over Barton Fell from Mr. Clarkson's, at the foot of Ullswater, towards Askam. The image of the hare I then observed on the ridge of the Fell.' The best commentary on the poem is from a letter written by Wordsworth to Sara Hutchinson on 14 June 1802:

'I describe myself as having been exalted to the highest pitch of delight by the joyousness and beauty of Nature and then as depressed, even in the midst of those beautiful objects, to the lowest dejection and despair. A young Poet in the midst of the happiness of Nature is described as overwhelmed by the thought of the miserable reverses which have befallen the happiest of all men, viz. Poets—I think of this till I am so deeply impressed by it, that I consider the manner in which I was rescued from my dejection and despair almost as interposition of Providence. "Now whether it was by peculiar grace A leading from above"— A person reading this Poem with feelings like mine will have been awed and controuled, expecting almost something spiritual or supernatural— What is brought forward? "A lonely place, a Pond" "by which an old man *was*, far from all house or home"—not stood, not sat, but "*was*"— the figure presented in the most naked simplicity possible. This feeling of spirituality or supernaturalness is again referred to as being strong in my mind in this passage—"*How came he here* thought I or what can he be doing?" I then describe him, whether ill or well is not for me to judge with perfect confidence, but this I can *confidently* affirm, that, though I believe God has given me a strong imagination, I cannot conceive a figure more impressive than that of an old Man like this, the survivor of a Wife and ten children, travelling alone among the mountains and all lonely places, carrying with him his own fortitude, and the necessities which an unjust state of society has entailed upon him. You say and Mary (that is you can say no more than that) the Poem is *very well* after the introduction of the old man; this is not true, if it is not more than very well it is very bad, there is no intermediate state. You speak of his speech as tedious: everything is tedious when one does not read with the feelings of the Author—"*The Thorn*" is tedious to hundreds; and so is the *Idiot Boy* to hundreds. It is in the character of the old man to tell his story in a manner which an *impatient* reader must necessarily feel as tedious. But Good God! Such a figure, in such a place, a pious self-respecting, miserably infirm, and Old Man telling such a tale!

'My dear Sara, it is not a matter of indifference whether you are pleased with this figure and his employment; it may be comparatively so, whether you are pleased or not with *this Poem*; but it is of the utmost importance that you should have had pleasure from contemplating the fortitude, independence, persevering spirit, and the general moral dignity of this old man's character.'

43. *Chatterton*: the fabricator of poems by a supposed fifteenth-century poet, Thomas Rowley. He committed suicide in 1770 at the age of 18. His 'Excellente Balade of Charite', in which the principal character is a needy old pilgrim, provided Wordsworth with the stanza for this poem.

45–46. A not very satisfactory characterization of Burns. He died in 1796 at the age of 37.

49. *despondency*: Wordsworth probably had Coleridge in mind, who had recently read him his 'Dejection: an Ode'.

56. After this stanza there stood another in 1807, which Wordsworth subsequently deleted in deference to Coleridge's criticism of its stylistic disharmony with its neighbours:

> My course I stopped as soon as I espied
> The Old Man in that naked wilderness:
> Close by a Pond, upon the further side,
> He stood alone: a minute's space I guess
> I watch'd him, he continuing motionless:
> To the Pool's further margin then I drew;
> He being all the while before me full in view.

57–63. The lines were quoted by Wordsworth in the preface to *Poems* (1815) to illustrate the modifying power of the imagination: 'The Stone is endowed with something of the power of life to approximate it to the Sea-beast; and the Sea-beast stripped of some of its vital qualities to assimilate it to the Stone; which intermediate image is thus treated for the purpose of bringing the original image, that of the Stone, to a nearer resemblance to the figure and condition of the aged Man; who is divested of so much of the indications of life and motion as to bring him to the point where the two objects unite and coalesce in just comparison.'

105. *an honest maintenance*: Dorothy Wordsworth records that, though the man's trade was to gather leeches, he no longer had the strength for it and 'lived by begging'. The theme of the poem required this to be modified.

PAGE 151. 'IT IS A BEAUTEOUS EVENING.' Composed on the beach near Calais.

9. *Dear Child*: Caroline, Wordsworth's daughter by Annette Vallon.

12–14. The child's unconscious acceptance of its heavenly inheritance is expressed again in the 'Ode to Duty', ll. 9–16 (p. 187), and 'Intimations of Immortality', ll. 66, 119–20 (pp. 182–3).

PAGE 153. 'SCORN NOT THE SONNET.' Wordsworth told Landor (20 April 1822) that he used to think the sonnet form 'egregiously absurd, though the greatest poets since the revival of literature have written in it. Many years ago my sister happened to read to me the sonnets of Milton . . . I was singularly struck with the style of harmony, and the gravity, and republican austerity of those compositions. In the course of the same afternoon I produced 3 sonnets, and soon after many others.' Wordsworth pays tribute to three Italian and one Portuguese poet (Camöens) whose eminence lies essentially in other fields, and the same may be said of the English poets chosen. The sonnet had regained favour during Wordsworth's life-time, after more than a century's neglect. It was Wordsworth and Coleridge who first drew attention to the merits of Shakespeare's sonnets.

PAGE 153. 'I WANDERED LONELY AS A CLOUD.' An extract from Dorothy Wordsworth's Journal, reprinted in Appendix, p. 215, records the occasion of the poem, and serves to illustrate the process of selection by the poet from the experiences of the day.

7–12. This stanza was added in 1815.

21–22. These lines were by Mrs. Wordsworth, and were thought by Wordsworth to be 'the two best lines' in the poem. They are in accordance with a view he had long ago expressed to Dorothy Wordsworth (6 Sept. 1790): 'At this moment, when many of these landscapes are floating before my mind, I feel a high enjoyment in reflecting that perhaps scarce a day of my life will pass in which I shall not derive some happiness from these images.'

PAGE 154. WRITTEN IN MARCH. Brotherswater is a small lake lying a few miles south of Ullswater at the foot of the Kirkstone Pass.

15. *anon*: 'now again'.

PAGE 155. TO THE CUCKOO. The cuckoo is a migrant that returns to the British Isles in spring. Wordsworth brushes aside the bird's traditional associations (with half-wits and the husbands of deceitful wives) to endow it here and elsewhere (see p. 168, l. 14) with mystery. He remarks in his *Guide to the Lakes* that there is 'an imaginative influence in the voice of the cuckoo, when the voice has taken possession of a deep mountain valley'.

4. *but a wandering voice*: the cuckoo is almost perpetually heard, but seldom seen.

5-8. This verse was perfected, after many attempts, only in 1845.

PAGE 157. 'I GRIEVED FOR BUONAPARTÉ.'

5-6. The same point was to be made in the 'Song at the Feast at Brougham Castle', ll. 157-60 (p. 177).

9-14. The overriding importance of humbleness and tenderness of heart in warrior or in statesman is often mentioned by Wordsworth. Compare 'Song at the Feast of Brougham Castle', ll. 165-70 (p. 177); 'The Happy Warrior', ll. 57-64; and *The Prelude*, XIV. 225, where it is declared that the man

> whose soul hath risen
> Up to the height of feeling intellect
> Shall want no humbler tenderness; his heart
> Be tender as a nursing mother's heart;
> Of female softness shall his life be full,
> Of humble cares and delicate desires,
> Mild interests and gentlest sympathies.

PAGE 157. ON THE EXTINCTION OF THE VENETIAN REPUBLIC. Napoleon entered Venice on 16 May 1797, and proclaimed the end of the Republic.

1. As a result of the Crusades, Venice had acquired territory in Asia Minor in the twelfth century. *in fee*: in absolute and rightful possession.

2. *the safeguard of the west*: from the power of the Turk after the fall of Constantinople in 1453.

7–8. Alluding to the annual ceremony on Ascension Day, when the Doge espoused the Adriatic by dropping a ring into the sea.

9–10. The power of Venice had been gradually declining since 1500.

11–14. For another instance of regret at the destruction of human grandeur, see p. 207.

PAGE 158. TO TOUSSAINT L'OUVERTURE. Toussaint (*c.* 1746–1803), surnamed L'Ouverture, became commander-in-chief of the forces in the island of San Domingo in 1796, liberated it from the French, and was named president; but he was captured and brought to France, where he died in prison.

PAGE 159. THOUGHT OF A BRITON ON THE SUBJUGATION OF SWITZERLAND. Napoleon invaded Switzerland in 1798 and again in 1802. Wordsworth thought this the best sonnet he had written.

PAGE 159. LONDON, 1802. The Peace of Amiens (March 1802 to May 1803) had enabled Wordsworth to pay a visit to France. On his return he recorded how he 'could not but be struck . . . with the vanity and parade of our country, especially in great towns and cities, as contrasted with the quiet, and I may say the desolation, that the revolution had produced in France'. This was one of the sonnets written to warn men of 'the mischief engendered and fostered among us by undisturbed wealth'.

PAGE 162. INDIGNATION OF A HIGH-MINDED SPANIARD.   Since 1800 Spain had been falling under French domination. Napoleon had sent more and more troops for the conquest of Portugal, and by 1808 the nature of his invasion had been recognized. This prompted patriotic risings, which with British assistance succeeded in restoring national independence in 1814. Wordsworth had watched this struggle with 'a depth of feeling not easy to conceive'.

PAGE 162. LINES COMPOSED AT GRASMERE. Charles James Fox, the political opponent of Pitt, died on 13 September 1806 at the age of 57. Wordsworth had sent him a copy of *Lyrical Ballads* in 1801, feeling assured that Fox would respond to 'Michael' and other poems because 'the whole of your public conduct has in one way or other been directed to the preservation of this class of men'.

PAGE 164. YARROW UNVISITED. Yarrow Water rises in St. Mary's Loch and runs north-east and east to join the river Tweed a few miles north-east of Selkirk. Besides 'The Braes of Yarrow' (1724), a poem 'in imitation of the ancient Scottish manner' by William Hamilton of Bangour, and another imitation by John Logan with the same title (1781), Wordsworth may have known two traditional ballads, 'The Dowie Dens o' Yarrow' and 'Willie's Drowned in Yarrow'. In the first three, *Yarrow* is the rhyming word of almost every stanza. Wordsworth's stanza was consciously adopted from another poem about Yarrow, 'Leader Haughs', printed in Ramsay's *Tea-Table Miscellany* (1724).

5. William and Dorothy Wordsworth were returning from a six-weeks' tour in Scotland. At Clovenfords they might have turned due south and reached Yarrow at Selkirk, six miles away.

6. *Marrow*: companion.

17. The Gala Water joins the Tweed three miles east of Clovenfords; the Leader Water is the next valley. *Haughs* is a north-country word for river-side meadows.

19. Dryburgh, with its picturesque ruined abbey, lies on the Tweed a few miles below its junction with the Leader. See p. 208, l. 10.

20. *lintwhite*: the linnet. Wordsworth recalls 'Leader Haughs':

> The lintwhite loud, and Progne proud
> With tuneful throats and narrow,
> Into St. Leonard's banks they sing
> As sweetly as in Yarrow.

21. The Teviot is the Tweed's next tributary on its eastward course.

33. *holms*: river-side meadows.

35. Wordsworth's note shows that he recalled these lines from Hamilton of Bangour's poem:

> Sweet smells the birk, green grows, green grows the grass,
> Yellow on Yarrow's bank the gowan,
> Fair hangs the apple frae the rock,
> Sweet the wave of Yarrow flowan.

37. *Strath*: a wide valley.

42. *Burn-mill*: Wordsworth recalled the name from 'Leader Haughs'. It is not in Yarrow.

PAGE 167. THE SOLITARY REAPER. Suggested by the following sentence in Thomas Wilkinson's *Tours to the British Mountains*: 'Passed a female, who was reaping alone: she sung in Erse, as she bended over her sickle; the sweetest human voice I ever heard: her strains were tenderly melancholy, and felt delicious long after they were heard no more.'

14. *the cuckoo-bird*: see p. 230, note on 'To the Cuckoo'.

PAGE 168. YARROW VISITED. See p. 165, ll. 49-55. Wordsworth feared that there was some falling off in this sequel to 'Yarrow Unvisited', since 'imagination almost always transcends reality'; but Lamb assured him that 'no lovelier stanza [than ll. 41–48] can be found in the wide world of poetry'.

25–40. Wordsworth recalls the story of 'The Dowie Dens of Yarrow', a ballad printed in Scott's *Minstrelsy of the Scottish Border*; but 'the Water-wraith' (l. 31) comes from Hamilton of Bangour's version. See p. 164.

55. *Newark's Towers*: a ruin on the banks of Yarrow three miles from Selkirk; the scene of Scott's *Lay of the Last Minstrel*.

PAGE 172. SONG AT THE FEAST OF BROUGHAM CASTLE. The ruins of Brougham Castle overlook the river Eamont, three miles south-east of Penrith. The story of Henry, Lord Clifford, was told by Wordsworth in a note to the poem. His father, a Lancastrian chieftain, had been slain at the Battle of Towton (1461) in the Wars of the Roses, and he 'was deprived of his estate and honours during the space of twenty-four years; all which time he lived as a shepherd in Yorkshire, or in Cumberland'. He was restored to his own on Henry VII's accession (1485). 'It is recorded that, "when called to Parliament he behaved nobly and wisely; but . . . rather delighted to live in the country" ', where he repaired several of his decaying castles.

6. *the red rose*: the emblem of the House of Lancaster.

7. *thirty years*: the period of the Wars of the Roses, 1455–85.

13. The House of York, whose emblem was the white rose, was 'blended' with the House of Lancaster, by the marriage of Elizabeth of York, daughter of Edward IV, to Henry VII.

25. *Bosworth-field*: the final battle of the Wars, in which Richard III was defeated and slain.

27. Wordsworth records taking this line from Sir John Beaumont's poem, *Bosworth Field* (1629).

36–46. All castles mentioned belonged to the Cliffords. Skipton is in Yorkshire, near Leeds; Pendragon and Appleby (l. 46) on the Eden; Brough on the 'humble' Swindale, all in Westmorland.

73, 89, 90, 92, 95, 123. The place-names mentioned all lie close to Saddleback (Blencathra), a mountain on the north-eastern edge of the Lake District.

122. There was a popular superstition that two immortal fish lived in this small lake, or 'tarn'.

157–60. See p. 230, note on 'I grieved for Buonaparté', ll. 9–14.

PAGE 177. YEW-TREES. Lorton lies four miles south of Cockermouth at the extreme north-west of the Lake District.

5. The Umfravilles were lords of Redesdale in West Northumberland in the thirteenth and fourteenth century. The Percys, earls of Northumberland, are chiefly associated with the east of the county.

7–8. Wordsworth mentions three battles at which English bowmanship gained the victory over French chivalry.

14. Borrowdale is a valley that runs due south from Keswick. These great yew trees which lie half a mile north of the village of Seathwaite were severely damaged in a storm of 1888.

33. Glaramara is a mountain at the head of Borrowdale.

PAGE 179. 'MY HEART LEAPS UP.'

9. *natural piety*: piety is the love and respect we naturally owe to our parents. Wordsworth owes it to his childhood, to which he is still bound by the same response to this great phenomenon of nature.

PAGE 179. ODE: INTIMATIONS OF IMMORTALITY. The first four stanzas were written in March 1802; the remainder were completed in March 1804. The sub-title was added in response to a request for guidance about the drift of the poem.

23. *a timely utterance*: perhaps the poem 'My heart leaps up' (p. 179), from which the epigraph is taken.

58–65. Wordsworth seems to have met this Platonic notion in Coleridge's 'Sonnet composed on a Journey Homeward; the Author having received Intelligence of the Birth of a Son' (1796):

> Oft o'er my brain does that strange fancy roll
>   Which makes the present (while the flash doth last)
>   Seem a mere semblance of some unknown past,
> Mixed with such feelings, as perplex the soul
> Self-questioned in her sleep; and some have said
>   We lived, ere yet this robe of flesh we wore.

Coleridge himself attributed the notion to Fénelon, whose followers 'believe that men are degraded Intelligences who had all once existed together in a paradisiacal or perhaps heavenly state. The first four lines express a feeling which I have often had.'

119–21. Wordsworth notes that 'nothing was more difficult for me in childhood than to admit the notion of death as a state applicable to my own being. . . . My difficulty came . . . from a sense of the indomitableness of the spirit within me.' At this point there followed three lines in the early editions:

> To whom the grave
> Is but a lonely bed without the sense or sight
> Of day or the warm light,
> A place of thought where we in waiting lie.

This characteristically Wordsworthian notion was omitted from later editions in deference to the objection that Coleridge had expressed in *Biographia Literaria* to the 'frightful notion of lying *awake* in the grave'.

142–3. Wordsworth told a friend that 'he used to be frequently so rapt into an unreal transcendental world of ideas that the external world seemed no longer to exist in relation to him, and he had to convince himself of its existence *by clasping a tree*, or something that happened to be near him'.

172. *in thought*: i.e. not spontaneously, but with the power of reflection brought by maturer years. Cf. l. 187.

176 ff. On the decay of rapture cf. *The Excursion*, IV. 123–40 (p. 197).

181. *what remains behind*: perhaps intentionally ambiguous: what survives from childhood, e.g. the 'primal sympathy' (l. 182), and what remains as a substitute, e.g. the 'soothing thoughts' (l. 184), the 'faith' (l. 186), the 'philosophic mind' (l. 187).

182. *primal sympathy*: *The Prelude*, I. 551–8 shows what Wordsworth meant (p. 50).

200. The two races are presumably the races of childhood and of maturity.

204. *Thoughts*: the emphasis from l. 169 onwards has lain upon the compensations of the mature man's reflections. Cf. 'Tintern Abbey', ll. 88–91 (p. 113).

PAGE 186. ODE TO DUTY. The composition of this poem intervened between the beginning and the completion of the 'Intimations' Ode, with which it is closely connected in theme. The stanza is taken from Gray's 'Hymn to Adversity', and in the phrasing there are several echoes of Milton. The motto is adapted from the 120th *Moral Epistle* of Seneca, a philosopher whose stoicism appealed to Wordsworth with increasing force. It may be translated: 'Not only sound in judgement, but so trained by habit that not only can he act rightly, he cannot help acting rightly.' The importance of Duty is more fully expounded in *The Excursion*, see pp. 195–8.

25. The remainder of the poem indicates his recognition of the change that has come upon him, and seeks to define what compensates for that which has been lost.

36. *the quietness of thought*: this is presumably brought by increasing years, like 'the philosophic mind' (cf. p. 186, l. 187).

41–48. Omitted by Wordsworth in all editions after 1807, but restored by later editors as a useful transition in the thought of the poem.

53–56. Other modes of being are subservient, gladly it would seem, to a spirit which impels them, as it impels the poet too. Compare *The Prelude*, II. 401–2 (p. 54), and *The Excursion*, IX. 238–40 (p. 201).

PAGE 189. ELEGIAC STANZAS. Peele Castle lies a little south of Barrow-in-Furness, North Lancashire. The picture by Sir George Beaumont (1753–1827), an artist friend of Wordsworth, who instigated the foundation of the National Gallery, was reproduced in Wordsworth's *Poems*, 1815, vol. 2.

2. *Four summer weeks*: Wordsworth refers to his visit to Rampside close by in 1794.

14–16. *add the gleam . . . Poet's dream*: revised in 1820 to read:

> add a gleam,
>
> Of lustre, known to neither sea nor land
>
> But borrowed from the youthful Poet's dream.

This is more readily understood (cf. *The Prelude*, II. 362–74, p. 53); but as a friend complained to Wordsworth, the original lines 'have passed into a quotation. . . . I don't see what right you have to reclaim and clip the wings of the words'. So they were restored, and with them the sense of something sacred in the unspoilt vision of the young poet.

29. *the fond illusion . . .*: such a picture would have been true to his experience at that early age. He has now lost the creative power (l. 35) demanded for such an imaginary picture, but he endeavours to find compensation in what he has gained (ll. 36, 53–54, 57–58).

36. *A deep distress*: the loss of his brother John at sea in 1805. *humanised my soul*: he had already learnt to hear 'the still sad music of humanity' (l. 91, p. 113), but presumably without being personally involved.

40. *with mind serene*: an ambition frequently expressed; compare *The Prelude*, I. 349–50 (p. 44).

50. *the look . . .*: the castle has become the symbol of the poet's stoicism.

53. *farewell the heart that lives alone*: a renunciation of his favourite role of the Solitary.

PAGE 191. 'SURPRISED BY JOY.' Said by Wordsworth to have been suggested by his daughter, Catharine, long after her death, which took place in 1812 before her fourth birthday.

PAGE 192. THE EXCURSION, I. 871–970. Lines 871–916 form the conclusion of a poem called *The Ruined Cottage*, completed but not published in 1797, the conclusion itself being composed in 1795. It is a tale of unrelieved misery; but soon afterwards Wordsworth began to draft an appendix (ll. 917–70) interpreting the tale in different fashion. What remains of the cottage and its garden may appear desolate, but

> by contemplating these forms
> In the relations which they bear to man
> We shall discover what a power is theirs
> To stimulate our minds, and multiply
> The spiritual presences of absent things.

We shall acquire the 'habit by which sense is made Subservient still to moral purposes'; not an object 'but may read'

> Some sweet and tender lesson to our minds
> Of human suffering or of human joy,

and we shall recognize the 'chain of good' that links us 'to our kind'.

> Thus deeply drinking in the soul of things
> We shall be wise perforce, and we shall move
> From strict necessity along the path
> Of order and of good.

This 'necessitarian' (see note to IX. 87, below) introduction to ll. 917 ff. was subsequently removed without radically altering the Pedlar's interpretation. The passage was accommodated to Christian principles in 1845, when ll. 934–9 replaced the single line 'Be wise and chearful, and no longer', and 'that could maintain . . . Faith' (ll. 952–5) replaced 'that could not live Where meditation was'.

IV. 66–139. The Wanderer 'acknowledges the difficulty of a lively faith', and faces some of the consequences of growing up: the loss of vision in childhood and young manhood, and the need of cultivating stoicism.

IX. 44–92. Wordsworth attempts to discover the compensations of old age, or, in the words of the 'Argument' to this Book, 'the dignity, powers, and privileges of Age asserted'. In his earlier work he had never felt the need of being 'disencumbered from the press Of near obstructions' (l. 70) in order to 'commune with the invisible world' (l. 86).

87. Compare a phrase from a notebook he kept at Alfoxden: 'They rest upon their oars, Float down the mighty stream of tendency.' It is not inconsistent with Godwin's doctrine of inevitable progress towards a state of perfection.

206–54. The passage, which begins with an affirmation of 'joy in widest commonalty spread' ('Prospectus', l. 18, p. 39), ends with a reaffirmation of the doctrine of the 'Ode to Duty'.

PAGE 202. COMPOSED UPON AN EVENING OF EXTRAORDINARY SPLENDOUR AND BEAUTY. The last of the visionary poems prompted by 'that blessed mood, in which . . . we see into the life of things'. The experience is now interpreted in Christian terminology; note, particularly, ll. 73, 76.

33. *purpureal*: a Latinism; equivalent to 'brilliantly coloured'.

61. *such hues . . .*: cf. 'Intimations of Immortality', ll. 1 ff., p. 179.

74. *Full early lost, and fruitlessly deplored*: ibid., ll. 66 ff.

PAGE 205. AFTER-THOUGHT. The series of sonnets prompted by the River Duddon ends with expressing a hope that the poet's life might terminate like the river, which flows after a boisterous course from the Cumberland hills 'over smooth flat sands' into the Irish Sea:

> And may thy Poet, cloud-born Stream! be free—
> The sweets of earth contentedly resigned,
> And each tumultuous working left behind
> At seemly distance—to advance like Thee;
> Prepared, in peace of heart, in calm of mind
> And soul, to mingle with Eternity!

To these somewhat commonplace reflections this is the magnificent 'afterthought'. For another expression of the idea of form persisting through change, see p. 195, ll. 73 ff.

PAGE 206. INSIDE OF KING'S COLLEGE CHAPEL, CAMBRIDGE.

1. *the royal Saint*: Henry VI, founder of King's College. The chapel was built between 1446 and 1515, and is the finest specimen of late medieval work in England.

9–10. *that branching roof Self-poised*: the roof is stone, groined, with fan-tracery, and unsupported by any central pillars.

PAGE 206. MUTABILITY.

14. This line also appears in an early fragment of a gothic tale (*c.* 1791) by Wordsworth in a similar context:

> The unimaginable touch of time
> Or shouldering rend had split with ruin deep
> Those towers that stately stood . . .;

and both passages were probably suggested by John Dyer's *The Ruins of Rome* (1740), ll. 38–42, which he considered 'a beautiful instance of the modifying and investive power of imagination':

> The pilgrim oft
> At dead of night, 'mid his oraison hears
> Aghast the voice of time, disparting towers,
> Tumbling all precipitate down-dashed,
> Rattling around, loud thundering to the moon.

PAGE 207. WHILE ANNA'S PEERS, &c. Suggested by the experience of a bed-ridden friend, Maria Jane Jewsbury (1800–33); yet the experience is not essentially different from that which prompted 'The Reverie of Poor Susan' (p. 134).

PAGE 207. AIREY-FORCE VALLEY. 'Force' is a north-country word for a waterfall. The Aira enters a deep, rocky, and wooded ravine, making a fall of 80 feet, shortly before it flows into Ullswater from the west, about half-way between the head and foot of the lake. The poem was classified by Wordsworth amongst 'Poems of the Imagination', perhaps by virtue of ll. 11–16.

PAGE 208. EXTEMPORE EFFUSION UPON THE DEATH OF JAMES HOGG. Verses written extempore immediately after hearing of Hogg's death, 21 November 1835. Hogg was an uneducated peasant of genius, who helped Scott in collecting materials for *Minstrelsy of the Scottish Border*. His best poem is *The Queen's Wake* (1816).

Verse 1. Wordsworth first visited Yarrow in September 1814, see p. 168. The Ettrick valley lies a few miles further south.

5. *When last . . . I wandered*: in September 1831.

8. *the Border-minstrel*: Sir Walter Scott, who lived at Abbotsford, about 10 miles away.

9–10. Scott died on 21 September 1832, and was buried in the ruins of Dryburgh Abbey on the River Tweed.

11. *braes*: the steep banks bordering a river valley. A north-country word.

15. Coleridge died on 25 July 1834.

19. Charles Lamb died on 27 December 1834.

25. *Yet I . . .*: Wordsworth was born in 1770, the same year as Hogg. He was seventeen months older than Scott, two years older than Coleridge, and five years older than Lamb.

32. *Hampstead's breezy heath*: a large open space lying a few miles to the north-west of London and still commanding a fine view of the city.

In 1817 Crabbe paid the first of many annual visits to London from his rectory at Trowbridge, Wiltshire. He stayed in Hampstead at the house of Samuel Hoare.

34. *Thou too art gone*: Crabbe died on 3 February 1832, in his 78th year.

37. *that holy Spirit*: Mrs. Felicia Hemans, poetess, died on 16 May 1835, aged 42.